EARLY CHILDHOOD EDUCATION SERIES
Leslie R. Williams, Editor
Millie Almy, Senior Advisor

ADVISORY BOARD : Barbara T. Bowman, Harriet K. Cuffaro,
Doris Fromberg, Celia Genishi, Alice Sterling Honig,
Elizabeth Jones, Gwen Morgan, David Weikart

looking at children's play

A BRIDGE BETWEEN THEORY AND PRACTICE

Patricia Monighan-Nourot
Barbara Scales
Judith Van Hoorn

with

Millie Almy

TEACHERS
COLLEGE
PRESS

TEACHERS COLLEGE, COLUMBIA UNIVERSITY
NEW YORK AND LONDON

Published by Teachers College Press, 1234 Amsterdam Avenue, New York, NY 10027

Library of Congress Cataloging-in-Publication Data

Looking at children's play.

    Bibliography: p.
    Includes index.
    1. Play—United States. 2. Child development—United States. 3. Educaton, Preschool—United States. I. Monighan-Nourot, Patricia, 1947– . II. Scales, Barbara, 1930– . III. Van Hoorn, Judith Lieberman.
LB1137.L66 1987   155.4'18   87-7139

ISBN 0-8077-2873-X
ISBN 0-8077-2872-1 (pbk.)

Manufactured in the United States of America

92 91 90 89 88 87   1 2 3 4 5 6

contents

acknowledgments

We wish to thank those who have provided us with inspiration and critical review of innumerable drafts, not the least of whom have been our co-authors. Friends and professional colleagues who have contributed welcomed assistance at critical junctures include Jane Hunt, Katie Danforth, Hannah Sanders, Joan Henry, Dorothy Eichorn, Naomi Caspe, Keith Alward, Kathy Sparrow, Ellen Richardson, Lisa Kirkup, Miriam Petruck, and Lori Mohan.

Millie Almy has enriched our lives personally as well as professionally. All of us have greatly appreciated her unflagging support and guidance. She is, of course, included with our mentors who helped us in the research process: John Ogbu, John Watson, Phil Cowan, John Gumperz, Anthony Stigliano, and John Clausen.

We are grateful to assistants who helped carry out the research: Betty Chan, Sandra Lepe, Charito Lopez, Barbara Villere, Charlene McNally, Gary Winston, Michael Miller, Bonnie Schreiter, and Beth Lewis. They provided the extra eyes and ears — and, in some cases, fluency in other languages — that allowed us to finish our work in a timely manner.

The patience of our secretaries and typists, Carol Sarnoff, Alice Engle, Kathleen Turner, Marcy McGaugh, and Patrice Parame, must be saluted. We appreciate the cooperation of Ablex Publishing Corporation and Viking Penguin, Inc., who granted permission to reprint materials.

We owe a special debt to the children and families who participated in our studies.

Finally, we want to acknowledge the forbearance of our families and friends, who have waited patiently for our return from the play yard.

looking at
children's play

A BRIDGE BETWEEN THEORY AND PRACTICE

1
introduction: defending play

For many years play has been the centerpiece of most early childhood programs. The place of play in the curriculum of the nursery school and how play reflects and bolsters the development of children has been a persistent theme in the literature of early childhood education. In the 1920s and 1930s, when the nursery school was still a new idea in the United States as well as in England, Susan Isaacs based her books *Intellectual Growth in Young Children* (1930/1966) and *Social Development in Young Children* (1933) on her systematic observations in the nursery school she directed. Across the United States in nursery schools situated at such institutions as the University of California at Berkeley, Iowa University, Yale University, Columbia University's Teachers College, and Bank Street College in New York, researchers, who were sometimes teachers, studied children's development and watched their play.

How the first nursery-school teachers, and indeed, the long line of early childhood teachers who followed them, felt about play was well expressed by Susan Isaacs when she wrote in 1929 that adults need to recognize

> how large a value children's play has for all sides of their growth. How great an ally the thoughtful parent can find it! And how fatal to go against this great stream of healthy and active impulse in our children! That "restlessness" and inability to sit still; that "mischievousness" and "looking inside" and eternal "Why?"; that

indifference to soiled hands and torn clothes for the sake of running and climbing and digging and exploring — these are not unfortunate and accidental ways of childhood which are to be shed as soon as we can get rid of them. They are the glory of the human child, his human heritage. They are at once the representatives in him of human adventurousness and hard-won wisdom, and the means by which he in his turn will lay hold of knowledge and skill, and add to them. (Smith, 1985, pp. 116–117)

How many early childhood teachers today would feel comfortable speaking to parents, or to their administrators and public school colleagues in such terms? What has happened to play and its defenders in the last half century?

The fact that teachers feel obliged to defend play reflects some of the central cultural values of our society, especially those subsumed under the work ethic.

HARD WORK ALONG THE ROAD TO SUCCESS

In a country where individualism is a core value, and where the self-realization of the individual is believed to be rooted in hard work, play becomes mere diversion.

Ironically, parents whose ancestors or who themselves came here from cultures where celebrations, festivals, singing, and joy making assume much more importance than in traditional American society often seem most determined that their preschoolers not spend too much time in play. Their resistance to a curriculum based on play reveals their understanding of the American work ethic and its implicit derogation of some of their own cultural values.

Among middle-class young people, the strength of the work ethic seemed to diminish during the so-called "revolution" of the 1960s and early 1970s. Many parents at that time wanted preschools to promote play, self-esteem, and concern for others. But in the achievement-oriented eighties parents began to ask whether the preschools expected their children to work as much as they should.

For example, among young upwardly mobile parents, play of the sort described by Isaacs is often rejected in favor of whatever seems likely to make the children "super kids." Games that teach reading and math, frequently at the computer; sessions at the "kindergym" to enhance motor skills; instruction in swimming and in another language all tend to replace spontaneous play.

The trend toward programming children for early achievement has become sufficiently pervasive to attract media attention. (See, for example, Elkind, 1981.) A former nursery-school teacher and researcher of children's play asks, with good reason, "Where have all the players gone?" (Curry, 1986). Fortunately, some evidence of a counter-trend is also appearing. Not all parents are convinced that earlier is better. They are wary of the possibility of burnout, and they believe in the positive values of play.

Since in this country counter-trends have a way of replacing trends rather quickly, we may ask whether play is about to be restored to what we believe to be its rightful place in the early childhood curriculum. The answer depends on many factors, including the stance that early childhood teachers take toward play. In the past their attitudes have shifted with changing circumstances. Teachers' uncertainty about how best to safeguard play also reflects changes in the early childhood education enterprise since its beginning some 60 years ago.

YEARS OF CHANGE

Nursery schools were no sooner established in university and college settings than they experienced new challenges. Could not the provisions made for children there be extended to children of families impoverished by the economic depression of the 1930s? At the same time, could not elementary- and high-school teachers out of jobs be retrained to function as nursery-school teachers? Thus began what has been called the "democratization" of early childhood education. The federal government assumed responsibility for Work Projects Administration nursery schools and, during World War II, for Lanham Act Child Care Centers. Neither program continued, but both left their impact on early education and care as a few states considered similar programs. At the same time, many teachers and parents, for whom involvement in a university nursery school would have been unlikely, became interested in establishing nursery schools for more children.

The number of nursery schools grew slowly but steadily through the 1950s and into the 1960s. In most, the curriculum provided time and materials for the children's play, sometimes designated as "free" play, suggesting a lack of teacher intervention. By then, while the importance of the developmental view and of the teacher's observation were still emphasized in early childhood education textbooks, teachers often found it difficult to articulate the reasons for the emphasis on play in the curriculum. They no longer had the closeness to developmental researchers that had characterized many nursery-school teachers in the early days.

A salesman father, who hoped that his son's career would lie in the sciences, found the teacher's comment that "They learn through their play" not very helpful. Equally exasperating was "We teach the whole child." What other kind is there? The father did not understand the teacher's shorthand for "We are concerned with all the interrelated aspects of the child's development — physical, mental, social, and emotional."

Later on, in the early 1960s, the media highlighted the importance of early learning, drawing on the research of Benjamin Bloom and the theories of Jean Piaget as interpreted by Jerome Bruner and J. McVicker Hunt. As a result, many parents became more insistent that teachers justify the role of play in their programs.

preschools for poor children

Some parents had undoubtedly also heard of new experimental programs for disadvantaged preschool children, getting under way at various universities. These programs varied widely. Some closely resembled the "traditional nursery school" by including time, space, and equipment for play; others were organized more like elementary-school programs. In some programs concern for the children's intellectual functioning exceeded all else, but in others physical, social, and emotional development also mattered.

Meanwhile the federal government rediscovered early childhood education, initiating Head Start programs for the disadvantaged in 1965. Once again came the necessity to train staff who had had little if any preparation for teaching preschool children. Designed to be "comprehensive," Head Start's goals included the provision of health care and nutrition and an environment designed to further social competence and parent involvement to the greatest extent possible. Biber (1979) reflects on the program:

> On the surface, for quick reference, it has been called a "play" curriculum. Under the surface, it represents the enactment of specific developmental principles: action to precede symbol, the fantasy route toward reality, cognitive insights derived within the context of direct experience, enlarged power to understand as well as to act, built through the interaction of maturing selves and minds. It was not enough to create environments that would be protective, nurturing, and socializing; the stimulation of thinking, reasoning, generalizing was crucial to sound future development and functioning. (p. 156)

The program, despite funding inadequate to provide for more than 20% of the children eligible for it, has survived for two decades. Its curricula vary widely depending on the goals of the parents, but play remains an important element.

curriculum models

The establishment of Head Start also marked the beginning of an era of curriculum "models" in which the sponsors of experimental programs competed to have their model adopted for use in particular school settings. The models competed again when the children's functioning was assessed (most commonly on some standardized test) following completion of the program, and in some instances at intervals thereafter. Data from some programs are still being gathered; as we shall see later, some have unexpected results.

For our purposes, two points need to be made. One concerns what each model required from the teacher in justifying play's place in it. The second may perhaps be termed the "schooling" (or "dedevelopmentalizing") of the nursery school.

The models varied widely in their attitudes toward play. At one extreme were programs that emphasized the teacher's instruction. These programs did not include a play period or used play only as a reinforcement for task completion. Such programs require the teacher to know very little about play or development. (The teacher should, however, understand the principles of behavior on which the program is based.) In contrast, a model based on traditional Montessori ideas emphasizes the child's self-instruction in a responsive environment. The teacher does not justify play but requires a thorough knowledge of development, as seen in Montessori's system. (Most American Montessori schools do make provision for play.)

At the other extreme, programs that emphasize play in the program and believe that to a considerable extent the children's development is furthered in their play, place a heavy burden on the teacher. To justify its place the teacher needs to understand principles of development as they apply to each individual child's play. Consider again Biber's specifics about the "under-the-surface" aspects of a "play curriculum." Do these not demand a teacher who is at once knowledgeable and keenly observant, as well as intuitive, sensitive, and insightful?

The incursion of curriculum models shook up the field of early childhood education. For the first time since Montessori's playless program confronted the early nursery schools, the children's play, that pleasant source of refreshment and humor in which so many teachers delighted (except when the twos were too messy or the fours too obstreperous), was threatened. Thoughtful teachers read books, went to workshops, looked at their children's play with new questions, modified some of their procedures, and changed play environments. One suspects that the *laissez-faire* attitude toward play declined. At the same time some teachers were won over to a curriculum where dittoes, worksheets, and gadgets for children to construct "with a little help" encroached more and more on play time.

enter the elementary school

Such encroachment represents the takeover of the nursery school by the elementary school. It has strange and contradictory elements in it. In the first place, in the generic sense (there are many excellent individual elementary schools), the elementary school has not been notably successful in meeting the needs of children. Indeed, the experimental preschool programs described earlier came into being because so many elementary-school children in poverty areas were failing to learn. No one knows for sure what effect might have been achieved by redesigning the elementary schools to accommodate better the needs and interests of poor children. A limited number of exemplary elementary schools suggest the possibilities. Instead, in effect, the effort went into redesigning the children by having them start school at younger ages.

In the second place, many of the elementary-school materials being adapted by preschools offer little opportunity for the problem solving, critical thinking, or creativity that can occur during play. Instructions that emphasize counting by rote, circling items on worksheets, and drilling with flash cards seem mindless by comparison. However, in saying this we do not imply that the preschool should be devoid of basics for the "three R's."

A wealth of research in developmental psychology has shown how children construct the concepts that are basic to mathematics and science. Recent research derived from linguistics and communication reveals how the young gradually attach meaning to reading and writing. Some of the experimental programs initiated in the 1960s, as well as a few traditional nursery schools going back to the 1930s, have demonstrated how to provide support for these intellectual endeavors without depriving the children of opportunities for other kinds of development.

Unfortunately many of the critics of public education, and of preschools as they have expanded in number, either derogate or take no account of the body of child development that undergirds early childhood education. They want to go back to the "good old days" and the "basics." One suspects that the basic teaching they have in mind is not that which they received as children but that received by their great-grandparents.

Keliher (1986), in a provocative article, shows that the back-to-the-basics movement is not new. She traces its cycles backward to 1962, 1954, and 1933. As she analyzes its nature she suggests that the slogan had better be "*forward to fundamentals.*" Today's children will be adults of the 21st century, not the 18th century. We owe them the kind of education that will prepare them for the years ahead, not the years *behind* (p. 43).

TEACHERS BESIEGED

Early childhood teachers currently find themselves pushed in many directions. Many are too stressed by inadequate wages, long hours, inaccessible parents, minimal supplies and equipment, and overbearing administrations to give thought to play. Others, perhaps a majority, sense that a better understanding of the place of play in the curriculum, on both their own part and the part of parents and policy makers, could greatly enhance their teaching. They confront many situations related to play that they find aggravating, puzzling, or contradictory. Some examples follow.

> In one school system, at the beginning of kindergarten the Gesell Developmental Assessment is administered. One five-year-old who tests above the norms is placed in a kindergarten class of 30 children. The curriculum there is "no frills," strictly the three R's. Another child of the same age who tests below the norm goes to a prekindergarten class of 18 children, well equipped for play.

Does it seem that, while the second child is being enriched, the first may be deprived?

> In another system, the children and the teachers enjoy the High Scope Curriculum, a curriculum that is oriented to the developmental needs of individual children and provides many opportunities for their play. The parents generally approve. At the end of kindergarten the children take a standardized readiness

test that bears no relation to the curriculum and allows no credit for the variety of knowledge and skills the children have acquired.

Does this mean the teachers should modify the curriculum, or should they protest the tests?

The delegate agency in a Head Start program proposes to make some outdoor play space available to the children. It will require some money to put the space in shape for use. Some of the parents argue that the money would be better spent for indoor equipment, since "the children will only run around out there."

What shall the teacher contribute to the discussion?

A group of employed parents is planning to start a childcare center, "but one that has a rich program of art, music, science, and literature." Their early childhood education consultant has just shared with them the National Association for the Education of Young Children's Position Statement on Developmentally Appropriate Practice in Early Childhood (NAEYC, 1986). One mother says, "I notice that the statement says 'Children learn most effectively though a concrete, play-oriented approach to early childhood education,' and also 'learning activities should be concrete, real, and relevant to the lives of young children.' Those statements trouble me. I understand that 3- and 4-year-olds are limited in what they can comprehend. But I notice that, when I do let Kimitaki and his friends watch TV, they do understand a lot that goes on. They know who the good guys and the bad guys are. I don't want him to watch TV in the center, and I do want him to have time for play. But I don't see why he should be limited to the 'real' and the 'concrete' or the 'here and now' you talk about. Why can't they have fairy tales and myths and some real art, not just pictures of objects, and good music?'

How does the consultant interpret the mother's concerns?

A young mother with a charming, active, 8-month-old daughter asks a teacher what she can do to stimulate the child's interest and skill in reading. The teacher replies, "Read to her, and play with her. Enjoy nursery rhymes and games." Later the mother returns, saying, "I've had a wonderful idea. I'll buy her a teddy bear that has the rhymes on a cassette."

How does the teacher respond?

Miguel, 4 years old, paints a large butterfly. At the bottom left-hand side he carefully makes a well-formed capital B. He removes the painting from the easel and takes it to the teacher. She nods approvingly and as she writes his name and the date on it, says, "You painted a beautiful butterfly."

Why did she ignore the obvious B?

Protecting the child's right to play is no easy job. It goes far beyond setting up an environment where play can occur. It includes knowing a great deal. It means knowing what goes on when children play, so that the environment can, in a sense, grow with the children, both as a group and as individuals. It means knowing when and how to intervene in the play and when to stay on the sidelines. It means comprehending the limits of play, knowing when play is not enough, knowing when children need the satisfaction of accomplishment in the real world and when soaring on the imaginations of others is more appropriate.

Protecting the children's rights to play also takes the teacher, as an interpreter of play, to other adults, including parents, principals and directors, custodians, other educators, and policy makers.

Not an easy job! Especially when the teacher has so many other concerns: boots that stick, mittens that disappear, juice that spills, blocks that topple, lunch that comes too early or too late, and volunteers that don't come at all; angry children, sad children, hurt children, happy children, all needing attention; parents to greet and to call; lists to be checked, orders to be sent, reports to be written; computers to be monitored, songs, stories, and books to be chosen. The list goes on and on. And for too many, nagging in the background, concern over inadequate salaries and benefits.

Despite these demands, most early childhood teachers enjoy their work. Ironically, they sometimes find it difficult to explain what they do. Too often their questioners assume that they "only play with little kids."

NEW RESOURCES AND NEW IDEAS: TEXT OVERVIEW

This book, addressed to all early childhood teachers — both practicing and prospective, whether in preschools, childcare centers, kindergartens or primary grades — attempts to deal with the problems associated with play in a way that is both realistic and positive. In most of the discussion, early childhood is equated with preschools. Most of the research and reflection about play has been carried out within this setting. But early childhood education is not limited to preschools. According to the National Association for the Education of Young Children (NAEYC), early childhood programs serve children from birth to age 8. Although the research the authors present here deals with infants and children in nursery schools, the authors believe that their findings have implications for the age span 0–8 years.

Drawing upon their own teaching experience, the authors believe that the recent rapid expansion of the body of child development research provides important new resources for teachers who want to look more closely at and better understand their children's play. Chapter 2 draws selectively on this research, in discussing questions that teachers often raise about play. As early childhood teachers, we may be skeptical about the usefulness of child development research and theory. Too often the theories we encounter seem not useful in practice, "not applicable in my classroom." Then we resort, consciously or unconsciously, to that mixture of theory, myth, and personal experience that seems to work for us, identified by Katz (1975) as "ideology."

Some of our problems in applying child development theory to play stem from the nature of the theory itself. Fein and Schwartz (1982), distinguishing between theories of development and theories of practice, describe the former as "universalistic" and "passivistic." Such theories are concerned with the behavior change over time of "typical" individuals, for example, white middle-class males, or poor black females. They assume a relatively stable environment, sometimes described as "minimally adequate," and no special interventions.

In contrast, theories of practice are "activist," concerned with changing behaviors by changing environments and by intervening to influence behavior. Theories of practice are focused on particular individuals, from the perspective of a specified practitioner, as teacher, parent, nurse, or social worker.

The other side of the coin of dissatisfaction with developmental theories can be seen as the desire for a theory of practice. Such a theory of practice emerges, albeit tentatively, as teachers with some knowledge of developmental theory observe the play of children closely and reflect on both the children's and their own behavior.

Following Chapter 2 are three chapters in which the authors describe the processes through which they, as teachers, observed children and listened to parents, raised questions, and sought answers. One was involved in a Head Start home-based program. A second taught in a cooperative preschool, the third in a university child study center. In the beginning their research was informal, similar to the What-if-I-tried-this? approach that good teachers use, both on the spot, to support children's learning, or in reflection over the day's or the week's activities. As each of the authors reflected on her findings and read related literature, new questions arose and the research took new shape, becoming a more formal study.

The three studies reported in Chapters 3, 4, and 5 represent but a small sample of the kinds of research that can be done to illuminate the possible connections between theories of development and potential theories of practice related to play. In some respects the material is anecdotal, similar to what all teachers report from their classrooms. More details are provided than is customary in most research journals. The authors tried to include details that answered questions they had had as teachers.

The authors challenge you as readers to consider whether the kinds of questions they have raised also arise in the settings where you work. What questions would you like to raise in your setting? To what extent would the procedures used in their studies be applicable in your setting? What other procedures might you consider? Do you think the findings of the studies would be the same or different if you attempted to replicate them? The authors of Chapters 3, 4, and 5 were fortunate to be situated in settings where they found individuals who could assist them as their research grew in size and scope. Note, however, that they began with questions that could be investigated by a single teacher or, better, by two teachers collaborating.

As it turned out, Van Hoorn, Monighan-Nourot, and Scales were also fortunate in their association with one another. Even before they had completed their studies, they began to meet together on a regular basis. At these meetings they discussed their procedures, the snags they encountered, and the solutions they devised. But more and more they talked about play itself. They discussed the changes in their views about developmental theory and research. They puzzled over play's place in the curriculum at different levels of development and why it seemed increasingly difficult to maintain.

They agreed about the place of play as central to a developmentally based curriculum, but found differences in the specific ways they sought to implement their programs, in finding the "right" balance between play and other activities. More and more, they came to believe that the teacher's role is crucial. Fully aware of the diverse pressures teachers experience, they nevertheless came to realize that early childhood teachers are well situated to bridge the gap between developmental theory and teaching practice related to play.

The remaining three chapters of this book consider the opportunities and responsibilities early childhood teachers have for addressing directly issues related to play and also the rewards that accrue from doing so. Although written by individual authors, these chapters reflect the many hours the authors have spent together. They have confronted their differences, clarifying but not always agreeing on issues. Despite occasional weariness, they have thoroughly enjoyed the process. When they speak of the importance of teachers finding support among their colleagues, they know firsthand its value.

Chapter 6 deals with the teacher's responsibility for play in the classroom. It describes how teachers can build effective communication between home and school with regard to children's play and how they can use play to assess and support children's development. This chapter also presents an analysis of some of the intellectual processes that appear to be involved in play. With knowledge of these and with sensitivity to the social and emotional significance of the play, the teacher can make judgments as to how, when, and why to intervene or not intervene in children's play.

Much of Chapter 6 can be described as "how to," but its "how-to's" are not based on prescriptions or formulas. Rather, the chapter assumes that the teacher is an intelligent person who draws actively and critically on child development theory and research. He or she also takes note of and reflects on what happens in the classroom, modifying approaches and testing hunches in the light of that experience.

The remainder of Chapter 6 plays with the reciprocal nature of teaching and researching. It underscores the importance of teachers' active involvement in research if theories of development are to become more useful and if theories of practice are to evolve.

Chapter 7 moves outside the classroom to consider the broader consequences of teachers' having, or not having, adequate knowledge of developmental theory and, more specifically, an adequate theory of practice related to play. It relates these possibilities to the current low status of early childhood teachers and to the increasing demands for childcare and early education. The chapter maintains that, without an effective theory of practice, without evidence that early childhood teachers' attitudes toward play are based on knowledge rather than only on intuition and sentimentality, teachers will never achieve the professional status they desire.

We set out to write a book that would look at play from the teacher's view. As we contemplate what we have done, it seems that we have also written a definition of what it means, at least as regards the teacher's role related to play, to be a *professional*.

Chapter 8 is Janus-faced, looking back to what we have done and also forward to what might be. The issue of professionalism comes to the foreground. As is appropriate for a book on play, the chapter concludes with fantasy. We pretend that a solidly based theory of practice is emerging, and we ask, What new directions can we envision?

2
views from the bridge: teachers look at play

Early childhood educators have intuitively believed that play is important in children's development. Play has always been central in the traditional preschool curriculum. However, only recently has play become an area of interest to the psychologist-researcher. For example, in the 1970 edition of Carmichael's *Manual of Child Psychology* (Mussen, 1970), which is a reference work widely used by researchers, there was no chapter on play. Mentions of play, doll play, playfulness, and games were limited to two dozen of its 2,400 pages. In contrast, the latest edition of the manual (Mussen & Hetherington, 1983) includes a chapter on play with some 450 references, about 60% of them referring to work accomplished since 1970.

Hopeful teachers who turn to this literature for the "answers" will find that often the studies do not address their questions. We have organized this chapter around the three questions that teachers most frequently ask and have reviewed the relevant literature in order to answer them. The questions are

1. How can I tell if it's play?
2. How does play change as children grow?
3. Why do children play?

HOW CAN I TELL IF IT'S PLAY?

characteristics of play

What are the characteristics of play? Are the children in the following episodes playing?

Three-year-old Amy picks up an old telephone recently donated to the playhouse. She takes the receiver and holds it next to her ear, then returns it to the cradle on the phone. She carefully places her index finger in each of the holes in the dial. She then "dials" each number in order: 1, 2, 3, 4.

Alex, age 4, grasps a marking pen and slowly prints "A," "L," "E," across the top of his paper. He reaches the edge of the paper, so he squeezes an "X" in above the other letters. Alex reaches across the table for a new piece of paper, inadvertently marking on the teacher's thumb as she sits next to him. He looks at her thumb and exclaims, "It has a ball on it! The letter i!" He points to a small speck of ink over the line he has made on her thumb. They both laugh heartily.

Researchers as well as teachers ask questions about the nature of play. Agreements about definitions enable researchers to compare results from study to study and to establish agreement on what is being observed. Available theories tend to agree about certain features that distinguish play from other behaviors (Rubin, Fein, & Vandenberg, 1983). These include (1) active engagement, (2) intrinsic motivation, (3) attention to means rather than ends, (4) nonliteral behavior, and (5) freedom from external rules.

ACTIVE ENGAGEMENT. The zest that preschool children bring to their play is evident in their unwillingness to be distracted, as well as in their actions and verbalizations.

Five-year-old Megan is playing the computer game called *Sea Horse Hide and Seek*. She is controlling the actions of a cute sea creature who must avoid the larger, less benevolent fish. The seahorses are not eaten or killed; rather, they are carried off the screen, never to be seen again. Megan gently guides her creatures along. At the appearance of the predator, she whispers, "No, Blackie. Can't catch me." The shark approaches, and Megan presses the reset button. She has taken the uncertain fate of the seahorse into her own hands.

As children grow older and play becomes interiorized in daydreaming, the engagement of the child's attention is not as readily identified by the adult observer. Nine-year-old Carlos, sitting at the kitchen table and gazing out the window, may be actively engaged in a fantasy about climbing a snowy mountain; but, unless he verbalizes his thoughts to an observer, this feature of play may be too subtle to distinguish.

The question of how actively preschool children are attending to their play is an important issue for their teachers. The teacher, surveying the classroom and its activities, needs to ask how many children are deeply involved in their play and how many are engaged in desultory activities that may reflect little more than boredom. Children, like adults, have "low" days; however, what is in effect the intellectual withdrawal of too many children on too many days should be cause for teacher concern.

INTRINSIC MOTIVATION.   Intrinsic motivation is the genuine desire to be doing what one is doing. Consider the following examples.

> Nick sits down in an empty chair where the teacher and two other children are playing a lotto game. Nick asks, "What's this?" The teacher responds, "It's a Halloween lotto game." "I'll play," says Nick, as he listens to the teacher's brief instructions for playing. Nick listens, then turns over a card. He matches it to his board. On his next turn, he picks a card and comments, "Two bats. No, I don't have two bats."

> Jenny is running across the yard, arms outstretched, shouting to three other girls, "Ah! We're chasing boys! C'mon, let's turn into Wonder Women!" They form a circle in the sandbox and turn around in place three times at Jenny's instruction. As they complete their spins, Jenny holds her arms above her head triumphantly. "Wonder Women to the rescue!" she cries, and leaps out of the sandbox.

Intrinsic motivation is clear in Jenny's self-initiated activity of playing Wonder Women. However, Nick's desire to continue the lotto game that was planned by the teacher may also be intrinsically motivated. Even though he did not initiate the play, Nick's interest in the activity offered by his teacher becomes intrinsically motivated as he chooses to involve himself in it.

What factors motivate children to choose an activity? Most experienced teachers recognize the potential that novel experiences have to motivate children to active engagement. Children may be motivated to choose new playthings or activities because they offer a "new angle" on a familiar experience. For example, when giant Tinkertoys or Leggos are added to the available materials, they provide children with the opportunity to apply familiar constructive play skills in an expanded form.

Children may also use familiar objects or activities to offer a "secure angle" on a new and perhaps discrepant or threatening experience. For example, Seth played almost exclusively in the housekeeping corner, feeding and changing the diapers on a baby doll, for three weeks after the birth of his baby sister.

ATTENTION TO MEANS RATHER THAN ENDS.   In play, children are less concerned with a particular goal than they are with various means of reaching it. Since the goals are imposed by the children themselves, the goals may change as play progresses. Once a child knows how to solve a puzzle, he might then stack the pieces in new arrangements or use them as props in pretense play. For example, Martin, while involved in house play, rubs a toy iron over the top of a plastic cauliflower, saying, "I need to iron this to bake it." After carefully running the iron over all the surfaces of the cauliflower, he returns to what appears to have been the original goal, saying, "OK, we can eat now."

This shifting among alternative patterns of means and goals appears to contribute flexibility to the child's thinking and problem solving (Dansky & Silverman, 1975; Pepler, 1982; Smith & Dutton, 1979; Vandenberg, 1980). These new combinations may be accompanied by a sense of discovery and exhilaration. Miller (1974) borrows "galumphing," a term from Lewis Carroll's poem "Jabberwocky," to describe this. "Galumphing" with ideas lacks the smoothness and efficiency that characterize more goal-specific activity, but it is experimentation that may enhance creative thinking. Opportunities for "galumphing" are lacking in curricula that are programmed to have the child arrive at only "correct" responses.

NONLITERAL BEHAVIOR.   This feature, the defining characteristic of symbolic play, begins as early as the first year of life (Fein, 1975) and is a predominant feature of preschool play. Children transform objects and situations to conform to their play themes. For example, Darrell, playing in the sandbox, makes "cream of mosquito" soup. He adds small pebbles to several scoops of sand, saying that the rocks are the mosquitoes. After he has "cooked" the soup, he gives several children pebbles to use as "money," first to buy the "mosquitoes," then to buy the soup he has for sale. Darrell transforms the pebbles to meet the symbolic needs of his pretend scenario as he develops it.

The exercise of "make-believe" is thought to contribute to the child's later skill with hypothetical or "as-if" reasoning (Fink, 1976) called for in scientific problem solving. Make-believe may also contribute to the use of abstract symbols (Fein, 1981; McCune, 1985, 1986; McCune-Nicolich, 1981). Using pebbles for money appears to be related to the ability to use printed symbols to represent words. This is a basic prerequisite to reading (Pellegrini, 1980). In addition, as the child develops the understanding of symbolic transformations in pretend play, he contributes to his understanding of logical operations such as reversibility and conservation (Golomb & Cornelius, 1977; Golomb, Gowing, & Friedman, 1982; Saltz, Dixon, & Johnson, 1977).

FREEDOM FROM EXTERNAL RULES.   Often cited to differentiate spontaneous play from games with rules, this   feature presents something of a paradox. Although there are no externally imposed rules in the spontaneous play of preschool children, play has implicit rules in at least two senses. An example of the first is when sisters play at being sisters. This imaginary situation already contains rules about roles, about how sisters behave with each other (Vygotsky, 1967). Another illustration comes from a group of children playing veterinarian. The behaviors of the girl playing the role of veterinarian and of the boy who plays a German Shepherd dog with a wounded paw reveal their understanding of the rules pertaining to the role of the doctor and the role of the animal patient, as well as to their relationship.

Second, observational studies viewing children's play as communication (Garvey, 1977; Schwartzman, 1978) have revealed that children generate rules about entering the play situation, establishing and developing a plot, and assuming their roles. Teachers can observe not only the play but the behind-the-scenes negotiations that allow it to happen. An example of negotiation showing good understanding of the rules comes from two 5-year-old boys wanting to play the role of father. The first boy says, "I'm the father." The second boy says, "No. I am." First: "I want to be the father." Second: "OK. You could be the father and I'll be the grandfather. Then we can both be fathers."

Following rules and taking roles in play is a pleasurable, intrinsically motivated experience for children. In it, children learn to understand not only their own roles and the rules that define them, but also the roles and rules of others. Coordinating several roles in a dramatic theme may prepare the child to engage in simple games with collective rules as she approaches the primary grades. Such behavior engages children in a beginning understanding of the rules and roles of our society (Fein, 1984; Monighan, 1985).

some issues in the definition of play

Two issues related to the definition of play deserve further comment. Both have to do with defining play in the classroom context. One has to do with the experience from home and elsewhere brought to the classroom by the child. The other relates to distinctions between play and exploration. When one child announces, "I'm the Dad" and another says, "I'll be the big sister," we anticipate a scene drawn from home or the television. Shifting to the block corner, we see two girls silently stacking blocks, alternating turns. Do the blocks represent a building they have seen? Are they playing the role of construction workers? With only this much information, we don't know. Moving to the art table, a 4-year-old looks up from his watercolor painting and says, "See my birthday cake!" We know he has symbolized an experience in his painting, but can we call it play?

These and other examples common in classrooms cause problems in making definitions of activities, because researchers or observers may not know the entire context in which a play episode occurs. Teachers, on the other hand, are often privy to what preceded a particular play episode and what influences from the home or peer group may be reflected in the children's activity. When 3½-year-old Jane sits in the playhouse highchair whining and pounding the tray, an uninformed observer may see her behavior as immature. In contrast, Jane's teacher recalls the more typical play of several weeks ago when Jane led a group of her peers in enacting a dramatic rescue from a burning building. Jane now has a new baby brother, however, and her play at preschool reflects her efforts to cope with the changes in her life at home.

Just as the teacher's knowledge of children's home life provides insight into their use and understanding of play roles, it is important to distinguish when children are not playing but exploring. In exploration, children attend to an object that has new features for them. Exploration is guided by the question, What is this object and what can *it* do? On the other hand, in play the question is self-references — What can *I* do with this object? — and the answer is, Anything I wish (Hutt, 1971; Weisler & McCall, 1976). Exploration affords the opportunity to discover the features of an object or situation. Exploration becomes play when the child uses information about the object to meet her own dramatic or constructive play needs.

This distinction is an important one, not only in assessing the child's behavior but also in planning curricula. For the teacher, the question is, What is the appropriate balance between experiences that encourage exploration and those that encourage playing? For example, the electronic robot that emits sounds and lights up when certain buttons are pushed invites exploration as a complicated and novel object. Only when the child incorporates the robot as a companion in space travel who is subject to the child's interpretations of its electronic features does the activity with the robot fully become play.

There is some evidence (Hutt, 1971) that playing with an object before it has been fully explored may limit the child's discovery of its specific properties. For example, the teachers in one center noted that the children had never used certain hand puppets except in the way that the teachers had prescribed when the puppets were new. They noted a similar lack of exploration of the properties and possibilities of a roll-away game that had been introduced with specific instructions as to how the game was to be played. This balance is critical as new technological games and toys are introduced in the preschool. For example, in selecting software for the computer, teachers need to be able to evaluate how well such materials support both exploration and play (Forman, 1985).

Traditional elementary education relies heavily on accommodation to the features of the external environment, making minimal provision for children to play with the concepts that they are acquiring. In contrast, traditional early childhood education provides for both exploration and play. However, today some preschools seem overcommitted to novelty in the form of a new activity or new materials nearly every day, without allowing much time for either spontaneous exploration or play. Other preschools remain committed to play but make little provision for novel materials or their exploration. The balance of exploration and play, or the novel and the familiar, is an important issue for early childhood education.

HOW DOES PLAY CHANGE AS CHILDREN GROW?

Teachers have long recognized that the play of 2-year-olds differs from that of 3-year-olds and that they in turn play differently from 4-,

5-, and 6-year-olds. A 2-year-old sets the table in the playhouse with toy plates, silverware, and plastic food. His actions indicate that he is copying what he has seen in reality. A 3-year-old in the same situation shows less concern for the realistic nature of the props. A block serves as a cup and a Leggo becomes a bottle for the doll in her lap. She talks with her baby, producing crying noises or demands in a high-pitched voice. Four- or 5-year-olds can imagine the dishes and silverware and can take the roles of family members and weave plots around them. A telephone call from Grandma at the bus station is readily incorporated into the household activities. For these older children the focus is on the drama that is played out among the roles they have taken. A real "situation" is extended and elaborated, rather than reproduced directly. Plots often carry over from one day to the next and may be continued for months.

Researchers have made fine-grained analyses of the development of children's play. Some have looked at the cognitive aspects of children's play and some at the social aspects, while others have attempted to combine social and cognitive elements. A fourth focus has been on children's communication during their play. In this section we present some of the findings from this research. This information may assist teachers in assessing the play of children in groups and in setting expectations for the development of play as children grow older.

The bulk of the available research relates to dramatic play. Less research has examined sensorimotor play, constructive play, and games with rules. Early studies were mainly descriptive, most of them drawn from the observations of classroom teachers. Research that followed was more often conducted in laboratory settings. Much of it was guided by theory in child development, in efforts to focus on particular features of play as it develops. Drawing on the ideas of Piaget and Vygotsky, researchers studied infants and toddlers to see when and how pretense play begins. Recently a substantial number of studies have been conducted in natural settings such as preschools and daycare centers, rather than in the laboratory. This trend heralds a revival of the early descriptive studies based on teachers' observations. Much of the research both past and present has been conducted in middle-class settings and may not apply universally, although there is a growing body of research that addresses both class and cultural differences in children's play (Curry & Arnaud, 1984; McLoyd, 1980, 1982, 1983; Schwartzman, 1985; Smith & Dodsworth, 1978; Tizard & Hughes, 1984).

This section is organized around the sequence of development of play as described by Piaget (1962), who was the first researcher to develop a comprehensive theory of play based on observations of children in natural settings. Piaget's categories focus on how children of different ages construct and express meaning through play.

Early play is closely tied to what is available in the child's physical environment: The 2-year-old who sets the table in the playhouse uses the toy plates, silverware, and plastic food at hand. A year later, play involves more imagination: The 3-year-old who wants a bottle for the doll on her lap does not stop her plan for feeding the doll because there is no bottle. She substitutes a Leggo block. In this pretend play she controls the meaning of objects, gestures, and situations. This ability to use mental representations rather than taking the objects or ideas from the physical environment or immediate context is called *decontextualization*. Gradually, children employ an internal "plan" in their play as they use decontextualization to control meanings. The toddler who washes her teddy bear's face, reads to it, and puts it to bed is following a mental plan based on representing events drawn from her own experience. Older children's choices of substitute objects and roles played in predictable manners are evidence of this expanding "plan" of mental representation and symbolic transformation.

According to the theory of Piaget (1962), infant play progresses from sensorimotor activity to pretend or symbolic play at around 15 to 18 months. Two types of symbolic play — constructive and dramatic — predominate throughout the preschool years until the age of 6 or 7, when the third type of symbolic play — games with rules — begins to assume greater importance. Within this framework, each of these kinds of play can be considered as it reflects the child's growing capacity for increasingly complex mental activity.

sensorimotor play

Sometimes labeled *practice play* or *functional play*, this activity begins in early infancy. Infants who have acquired some pattern of action, such as grasping or looking, are now able to repeat these patterns (or *schemas*, as Piaget referred to them) just for their own sake. As infants grow older, they are able to combine these patterns and apply them to an increasing array of objects. Grasping a doll or a finger serves as an opportunity for activity or for play that is "a happy display of known actions" (Piaget, 1962, p. 93).

Infants' sensorimotor encounters with the environment are not limited to physical objects but include their caretakers as well. Some of these encounters become ritualized as combinations of sensorimotor actions, such as picking up a phone receiver and holding it to the ear. Such rituals signal the child's beginning awareness of her own actions and the imminent emergence of symbolic play. Sensorimotor play, however, does not disappear with the advent of symbolic play but remains as the foundation of more complex kinds of play (McCune, 1985, 1986).

Teachers recognize sensorimotor play in preschool and elementary-school children when they see them running for the sake of running, jumping up and down exuberantly, clapping one block against another, repeatedly pouring water or sand, or repeating nonsense phrases over and over. Sensorimotor play is also present in the behavioral repertoires of adults. The adult who jogs, dances, plays tennis, or doodles with a pencil is engaged to some degree in sensorimotor play.

During the preschool years such play declines with development only in its frequency relative to symbolic play. In studies reported by Rubin et al. (1983), sensorimotor play drops from 53% of all free activity at ages 14 to 30 months to less than 33% by age 5, and may comprise less than 14% of all play by the time children are 6 to 7 years old. Older children's play often combines sensorimotor and dramatic elements. Examples of this are the elaborate space chase games that combine the joy that comes from running, leaping, and crouching, enhanced with the excitement of an imagined flight with media characters such as My Little Pony or He Man.

Sensorimotor play beyond the infancy period has received limited attention from researchers. Most preschool teachers have experienced sensorimotor play at group or circle time. One child begins clicking her tongue or snapping Velcro fasteners and quickly the activity becomes a group phenomenon. Teachers would like to know more about the factors that precipitate such play and about the circumstances under which it becomes contagious. Does the child see it as different from other kinds of play that are looked upon more favorably by the teacher? To what extent is it an ingredient in rough-and-tumble play, in movement play, or even in dramatic play? Such information would enable the teacher to understand better both group and individual behavior in the classroom.

symbolic play

As the child's ability to use symbolic or mental representation develops, a shift is made from sensorimotor play to symbolic play. Children begin to detach literal meanings from sensorimotor routines to form abstract representations of such activities. They can now shift from actions centered on themselves to actions attributed to others as well. They are able to begin to integrate symbolic meanings into increasingly complicated sequences of play involving object substitution and role play.

Symbolic play, in its early forms in infancy through the preschool years, has been the focus of research in recent years. Researchers think that make-believe taps a variety of cognitive and social skills. Looking at forms of pretense play in the developing child, they observe characteristics that are also found in the thoughts of mature individuals: the decontextualization of the symbol, the shift from self-referenced to other-referenced action, and object substitution.

DECONTEXTUALIZATION OF SYMBOLIC REFERENT.   Decontextualization can be observed in the earliest pretend gestures of the infant at 12 or 13 months of age (Fein, 1981; McCune-Nicolich, 1981; Rubin et al., 1983). These pretense behaviors associated with eating, sleeping, or other familiar experiences are detached from the circumstances or contexts usually surrounding them. For example, the baby imitates sleeping behaviors when it is not bedtime or replicates drinking behaviors when there is no liquid in the cup. From the cognitive perspective it is "as if" the gestures have begun to stand for or symbolize the situation of sleeping or drinking. From the standpoint of social development, the child seems to have abstracted the basic qualities of certain situations such as where and how one sleeps and what one drinks and in what utensils.

SHIFT FROM SELF-REFERENCED TO OTHER-REFERENCED ACTIONS. Pretense play during the second year expands from exclusively self-referenced actions (the child drinks from the cup herself) to include other-referenced actions (the child has her mother or her doll do the drinking). Initially the child takes an active role and the doll serves as a passive recipient of the child's action (Overton & Jackson, 1973; Werner & Kaplan, 1964). Later, however, the child treats the doll as though it were the active agent, as if the doll itself were drinking from the cup (Fein & Robertson, 1974). These shifts in pretense behavior appear to form a developmental sequence (Watson & Fischer, 1980). From 12 to 30 months of age, children show a steady increase in the tendency to have the doll act as a separate individual.

Every teacher has favorite examples of children's developing ability to sustain the identity of a doll or even an imagined companion.

Four-year-old Barbara brings her Mickey Mouse doll to preschool. Mickey interrupts Barbara's conversations with adults and other children. Speaking in a high-pitched voice, he demands a drink of water or asks a question. Three-year-old Susan brings an imaginary rabbit to the center each day. She consults with the rabbit before selecting among the activities provided.

In role taking, the child must coordinate his or her own self-identity with the role of another (Gould, 1972) and then extend this into a sequence of familiar activities (Fenson & Ramsay, 1980; Fein, 1985a; Miller & Garvey, 1984). Role taking appears to be related to the more complex taking of the perspective of the other that is inherent in successful social relations and probably also in the solution of a variety of intellectual problems (Connolly & Doyle, 1984; Light, 1979; Mead, 1934; Rubin, 1982). It is this ability that we expect children to have when we ask the "hitter" how it feels to be hit. Although these relationships have not yet been firmly established in empirical research, the child's role taking does provide the teacher with clues as to the progress the child is making in both social and cognitive development.

OBJECT SUBSTITUTION. The child's ability to substitute one object for another (for example, a shell for a cup) has been of considerable theoretical interest in establishing the roots of symbolic behavior (Piaget, 1962; Vygotsky, 1962, 1967; Winnicott, 1971) and has been studied extensively (Fein, 1975, 1981; Rubin et al., 1983). Research by Fein and others indicates that, as children develop, their ability to substitute several objects in the same play sequence increases.

Follow-up studies have examined how the nature of the substitute objects affects the children's pretense. Children find object substitution easiest when the objects resemble the realistic object in form, as a shell resembles a cup, or in function, as a bottle resembles a cup. The child finds it relatively easy to assign an alternative function to an object with an ambiguous function, such as a block instead of a cup. It is more difficult to replace the cup with an object that has a conflicting function, such as a toy car (Elder & Pederson, 1978; Jackowitz & Watson, 1980; Pederson, Rook-Green, & Elder, 1981).

Young preschoolers (ages 2 and 3) may prefer highly realistic objects in pretend situations (e.g., a toy car versus a block). However, this preference shifts as children grow older (Fein, 1979; McLoyd, 1983; Pulaski, 1970; Suzuki, 1983). By age 5, nonrealistic objects such as blocks evoke richer and more varied fantasy themes. Children at this age indicate preferences for the objects that allow them to develop their own pretend schemes with a maximum of leeway for successive transformations with the same object:

> Meka offers a cardboard cone to Houston. "It's chocolate. Eat it before it melts." A few minutes later she uses the cones she has collected to make a wall around a cardboard block castle. Still later in the morning she uses a cardboard cone as a telescope to "sight land" from a ship and as a weapon to "fight off the bad guys."

Findings such as these raise many questions of interest to the teacher. For example, does the provision of realistic objects such as model farm animals or plastic replicas of food inhibit the play of older children? Might such replicas serve to facilitate the play of an older child who seems less imaginative than most?

The ways children use or don't use props in their play may provide interesting clues to their development (McLoyd, 1986). A parent reports her surprise at finding that her 4-year-old daughter prefers styrofoam packing chips to the realistic-looking plastic vegetables and hamburgers she had purchased for her playhouse. This points to some questions that may be asked regarding any child. Does the child require a prop to begin pretense play? How flexible is the child in transforming an object into a prop for pretending? Do the transformations appear to be planned or spontaneous? Are props really needed, or is the pretense of objects in the "mind's eye" alone sufficient? In the latter case, what about the actions of the child? Are they consistent with the object represented? Questions such as these may supplement the questions that teachers have traditionally asked about children's symbolic play and what it may represent in emotional as well as intellectual and social terms.

In addition to the characteristics of symbolic play just discussed, there are three different kinds of symbolic play: constructive, dramatic, and rule-governed play.

CONSTRUCTIVE PLAY.   Constructive play is characterized by the manipulation of objects to construct or create something. In contrast to play in which a child transforms a block into anything she wants it to be, in constructive play the block is used only as a symbol for blocklike objects such as houses or towers. These uses show that the child is using the object within the constraints of physical reality.

Piaget places constructive play midway between work and play. It is characterized by more imitation than dramatic play, which commonly involves role play and imagined themes. Constructive play is exemplified by the "engineering feats" of preschoolers using blocks and other such toys:

> Three-year-old Toshiko is sitting cross-legged, alone near the wooden dollhouse. She fits a piece of wooden train track onto four already connected. Then she adds one more piece, struggling to fit the piece on evenly.

Another type of constructive play involves symbolic constructions using paint, playdough, or collage materials to represent the child's own reality:

> Two-year-old Mark is at the playdough table. A mound of playdough in the baking pan is in front of him. Mark is putting toothpicks into the dough, vertically, one at a time. He holds the pan of dough up over his head with one hand, saying, "Here's my cake!"

From their examination of research in preschool and kindergarten classes, Rubin et al. (1983) report that "constructive play is the most common form of activity, ranging from 40% of all activity at 3½ years to approximately 51% at 4, 5, and 6 years" (p. 79). Tizard, Philips, and Plewis (1976), in a study of English preschool centers, suggest that the high proportion of constructive play may be an outcome of an environment that emphasizes the manipulation of objects and may inhibit symbolic activity. In contrast, Forman and Hill (1980) see the "open-ended playing around with alternative ways of doing something" as constructive play that "by definition builds on itself to increase the competence of the child" (p. 2).

But constructive or manipulative activity need not preclude imaginative activity:

> Four-year-old Miguel has built a three-tiered structure from playdough and has placed smaller pieces of dough around it, like stepping stones. Using a cookie cutter shaped like a man, he walks it around the structure, chanting, "I'm walking on the sidewalk!" Then he hops the cutter up and down in front of the structure. In a low, gruff voice he says, "Little pig, little pig, let me come in. I'll huff and I'll puff and I'll come in." Then he changes to

a high voice, "Not by the hair of my chinny-chin-chin!" In a normal voice he says, "Whoa! B-r-ck!" and crushes the playdough structure with the cutter.

Clearly, both constructive and imaginative activity are present in this child's play. As with the question of exploration versus play, a balance of opportunities for constructive representation and its expansion into dramatic sequences is the key here.

What seems to be needed on the part of both researchers and teachers is greater attention to what children do with the variety of objects they encounter in a preschool. Are their activities merely manipulative (i.e., is the play at a sensorimotor level)? Or are they symbolic in the sense of using the objects to create new objects or new effects? Or is dramatic activity also involved? When it is subjected to sufficient scrutiny, constructive play can be seen to have a place in the curriculum, overlapping with dramatic play, and it can be perceived to be equally as important.

DRAMATIC PLAY.   From the preschool teacher's viewpoint, the most common type of symbolic play is that labeled "dramatic play," usually occurring in areas set up with props designed to assist the children in depicting themes from their own experiences. As the example with Miguel at the playdough table illustrates, such play is not limited to those areas but may occur in conjunction with constructive play in the block area, or when the child is painting, using playdough or clay, or riding a tricycle.

Dramatic play involves the substitution of an imaginary situation for the immediate context. Children use mental representations of objects, situations, and behavior to coordinate the roles of self and others in a covert, implicit fashion in dramatic play.

> Four-year-old Peter approaches 4-year-old Marty and asks, "Are you Spider Man or are you the dog? I am 'ow ow ow'" (howling like a hound). Peter picks up a plastic hot dog with his teeth and carries it to Marty, who is kneeling, pretending to eat from a cardboard block.

When teachers observe children as they engage in dramatic play, they become aware of two key factors. One involves the social nature of such play. Pretend play may be solitary, but it also may include interactions among several children. Categories describing solitary, parallel, and group play behavior were first introduced by Parten (1932). Her work and some more recent studies indicate that as children develop they are more inclined to engage in group dramatic play. For example, Johnson and Ershler (1982) conducted a longitudinal study of children who were 3-year-olds at the beginning of their observations. They found a steady increase in both the amount of children's dramatic play and the maturity of their social interactions.

The second factor relates to the cognitive complexity of play in either solitary or group social contexts. The degree to which children are able to represent complex themes, roles, and objects in their play has captured the attention of researchers such as Smilansky (1968) and Rubin, Maoni, and Hornung (1976; Rubin, 1982). Smilansky uses the term *sociodramatic play* to describe play that is cognitively advanced. The highest level includes such elements as imitative role play, make-believe with objects, make-believe with actions and situations, persistence, interaction with at least two players, and verbal communication. Rubin has combined Piaget's categories of sensorimotor and symbolic play with the social categories of solitary, parallel, and group play. Teachers can draw on Smilansky's and Rubin's work as they think of the variety of transformations and interactions that go on in a play episode.

It may be possible to penetrate the intellectual complexities of play episodes more deeply. Further insight into the intellectual complexities of dramatic play comes from studies of the ways children communicate when they play. Garvey (1977), in observing pairs of previously acquainted nursery-school children, notes the ways in which children communicate that "this is pretend." She also notes the kinds of play episodes and roles they most frequently enact (Garvey & Berndt, 1977; Miller & Garvey, 1984). In order to negotiate dramatic play episodes children must understand the differences between real and pretend, establish implicit rules for communicating about their play, and contribute to an agreed-upon theme (Brenner & Mueller, 1982; Garvey, 1974; Giffin, 1984). Such analysis of children's dramatic play is useful for teachers who want to understand and support it as effectively as possible.

GAMES WITH RULES. This third type of symbolic play is characterized by the acceptance of prearranged rules and the adjustment of these rules throughout the course of play. Roles of self and others must be coordinated in an overt, explicit fashion.

Five-year-old Nathaniel is helping to organize a baseball game with four other children. He is standing near the garden with a ball in his hand, gesturing. "All right, whoever wants to play baseball, go to that tree. I'm figuring out the game. Now, don't fool around. Some of you guys can't catch well." He points to Miguel. "Now you're the pitcher. When I say 'pitcher!' you hafta get there" (pointing to a spot in the garden).

Group games such as Duck, Duck, Goose or simple board games at a preschool level require the understanding and adherence to specific, nonfluctuating rules and the use of strategy in order to "play" successfully. These components — consistent rule taking and strategy — require entrance into a realm of mental abstraction far removed from immediate physical objects and contexts. Games with rules assign symbolic meanings to vehicles (e.g., players, wood markers) that may be different from the physical properties of the objects to which they refer.

In the years from 4 to 7, children begin to be able to participate in games with rules. Such games arise out of sensorimotor combinations (races, ball games) or intellectual combinations (cards, board games) and are regulated either by a code that has been handed down or by mutual agreement. According to Piaget these games are also competitive. More recent cross-cultural work suggests that competition is defined differently in different cultures and that some cultures place more emphasis on collaboration and cooperation than on competition (Schwartzman, 1978).

Games with rules differ from pretense play in that the rules have been established in advance and determine how the play is to go. Any alterations in the rules must be agreed upon by the players beforehand. These predetermined structures contrast with the ad hoc negotiation and flexibility of dramatic play.

The literature related to games is voluminous, but little describes the way young children begin to acquire game-playing skills and gain understanding of games. A few exceptions are Piaget's (1965) early investigation of games with rules, which includes several 5-year-olds; and Kamii and DeVries's *Group Games in Early Education* (1980), a book that reports on the ways these two authors intro-duced such games in the preschool. Some recent work involving children's strategies with the computer shows promise in this area (Alexander, 1985; Clements, 1986; Fein, 1985b; Forman, 1985; Kee, 1985).

some issues in the development of play

The sequences of development in play have often been taken by teachers as guides to the maturity of a particular child's play development. Those given special emphasis have been Parten's (1932) description of the developmental sequence moving from solitary to parallel to cooperative, and Piaget's (1962) sequence from sensorimotor to symbolic to games with rules. More recent research (Bakeman & Brownlee, 1980; Monighan, 1985; Moore, Evertson, & Brophy, 1974; Rubin, 1982; Smith, 1978) indicates that two of these areas need especially to be considered when assessing children's play. They are solitary play and parallel play.

SOLITARY PLAY. The issue of solitary play in classroom settings is the first issue of concern. Early childhood teachers may recall from their textbooks that the play of 2- and 3-year-olds is often described as solitary, while that of 4- and 5-year-olds is described as associative and cooperative. As Hartup (1983) notes, this is an oversimplification. The frequency of solitary play among 5-year-olds does differ from that of group and parallel play at that age (Barnes, 1971; Monighan, 1985; Parten, 1932; Rubin, 1982). However, the important changes in social play during the preschool years are qualitative, as represented by older children's ability to sustain increasingly complex social interactions and symbolic transformations in their play. There is little reason to assume that solitary play is less mature than interactive play, or that children always benefit from admonitions to share their toys. Instead there may be good reason for the fostering of solitary play in the curriculum. The sense of mastery that children gain from solitary play appears to provide a solid base for the cooperative play, sharing of ideas, and social negotiation that are also called for in educational settings. The opportunity to consolidate intellectual activities in a private context may also contribute to the development of problem-solving skills and a reliance on self-control in educational settings (Moore, Evertson, & Brophy, 1974; Rubin, 1982; Singer, 1973; Wertsch, 1979).

Even when they are aware that privacy is an important feature of the preschool environment, teachers also have responsibility for the guidance and care of groups of children. The need to supervise, schedule, and allocate materials sometimes conflicts with the needs for children to play by themselves.

PARALLEL PLAY. The second issue has to do with the nature of parallel play, which, like solitary play, remains at rather high levels during the preschool years (Hartup, 1983). Closer attention from both researchers and teachers reveals that parallel play often involves social coordination of gestures, if not of verbal behavior. Parallel play may be used by skilled players both as a means of entering play or as a means of drawing others into play (Bakeman & Brownlee, 1980). Thus, it may sometimes represent greater social maturity than is implied in the usual definition of "playing beside, but not with" another child (Smith, 1978). Again, the problem that arises may be one of oversimplification, which should be avoided in the interests of giving children the full range of opportunities they need for growth.

WHY DO CHILDREN PLAY? THEORIES OF PLAY

Many teachers find theories of child development or research reports from the fields of psychology or education totally irrelevant in their classrooms, or with their children and families. Scores and averages and recommendations that begin by stating, "The child learns by . . . " seem a waste of time to a teacher who has more immediate concerns, such as a new sand table, no yellow paint, or a broken tricycle.

But in fact, consciously or unconsciously, we as teachers manage play and define time and space for it on the basis of theories of development. Notions about what it is that play does for children may reflect theories that are now regarded as "classic." Thus, the notion that "play lets the active child run it out" comes from the surplus energy theory, while "balance the academics with active play" reflects recreation theory. "They learn through their play" represents practice theory. "Play reflects the culture" has its roots in recapitulation theory.

The most direct influence on teachers' thinking about play probably comes from 20th-century theorists associated with psychoanalysis (Erikson, 1950; Freud, 1964; Isaacs, 1933, 1930/1966). Here the guiding ideas may be "children work out emotional conflicts in play" and "in play children develop mastery." Piaget (1962) also contributes to our current ideas of play, which include "play is involved in cognitive development," "play develops in stages," and possibly "play is assimilative; that is, it serves to incorporate or consolidate the child's experiences."

The views of several other theorists have also appeared in the literature of early childhood. Bruner (1972, 1976) sees play as "serious business," an important factor in evolution and development. Lieberman (1977) described "playfulness" as a personality trait, a component of imagination and creativity. Singer (1973) finds in make-believe play a process which "if it is gently fostered as a human skill can make life infinitely richer and more exciting" (p. 259).

Sutton-Smith (1971, 1979, 1986), who has served as a synthesizer of psychological and anthropological approaches to play, describes play as "performance." He places play in historical and cultural contexts and examines some of its inherent contradictions. For example, to play is to be free and to have fun, yet the content of the play often reflects situations that are filled with suspense, calamity, or even tragedy.

Current theories about young children's play are also drawn from fields outside of psychology. One example is the philosophy of George Herbert Mead (1934). According to Mead, play contributes to the progressive differentiation of "self" from "other" perspectives in the child's social world. An example would be for the child to understand her role as the "baby" and her friend's role as the "mother." Play also assists in the differentiation of the component parts of the self. For example, the child begins to differentiate the "I," or self as subject ("*I* have a train") and the "me," or self as object ("Jamie gave *me* the train"). These two elements of the self arise in the process of social interaction. As children develop and come to view their own behavior from the perspectives of others, the "I" and the "me" interact as the child plans and reflects upon activity.

For Mead the "I" is the part of the self that asserts its uniqueness in relation to others. It is the part in each of us that enjoys our own success and is the source of our novel and spontaneous behavior. The "me" in the self dictates appropriate behavior in social situations, masters conventional social gestures, and reflects on the behavior of the self from the perspective of others. For Mead, the young child is the naïve expression of the "I," as childlike behavior resonates with the "I" in each of us. The "me" is developed as the child masters the forms of the social milieu in which he operates.

Although Mead does not thoroughly describe the process of developing a sense of "me," he sees play as the basic activity in childhood that supports the development of a unified self with both the "I" and the "me" as elements. The "play stage" of self-development begins as children become able to symbolize experience internally. They also begin to take the roles of others with regard to themselves. Initially, they assume these roles consecutively, with no cohesive rules by which to unify the process. For example, 2-year-old Duane may play a lion, a dog, a truck, and his parent all within a 10-minute period. An observer would not be able to identify a single theme or coordination of roles.

The "game stage" of self-development is characterized by the child's ability to "take the attitude of everyone else involved in the game," and understand the relationship of these different roles to each other (Mead, 1934, p. 151). The child at this stage can sustain several perspectives (as well as her own) simultaneously and can coordinate these viewpoints in negotiating play with others. The child who plays the father in the family, answering the phone, cooking a meal, coordinating his pretend responses to the "daughter" and "grandfather" roles in the play, provides an example of Mead's "game stage." (See Fein, 1984, for additional examples of this stage.)

The third stage in this sequence Mead terms the "generalized other": the attitude of the whole community. The individual at this stage has internally symbolized the attitudes of nonspecific others, as expressed in rules or codes of conduct, and uses those to guide her behavior. The very beginning of Mead's "generalized other" stage is seen in children's first games with rules. A child playing hide-and-seek or checkers coordinates perspectives of self and others and adheres to a generally accepted set of shared meanings, expressed as rules.

Vygotsky (1967) sees play as an aspect of the preschool child's living in which he advances beyond the ordinary accomplishments of the age period and anticipates development in thinking that will only become characteristic later on. As Vygotsky puts it, the preschool child in play is "always above his average age, above his daily behavior." Accordingly, "play creates the zone of proximal development of the child" (p. 16).

The views of the anthropologist, Gregory Bateson, have influenced other theorists and researchers. Bateson (1976) has examined the significance of how humans communicate to each other — through a wide-eyed expression, a wink of one eye, or an exaggerated tone of voice — that they are in a state of play (i.e., "This is play"). In learning to tell others that an act is playful, the child finds that there is such a thing as a role and that the style in which a role is played depends on who one's fellow players are. For example, children's roles in pretend play often reflect their social standing. Mature children or those who are leaders of their peers are likely to play high-status roles such as parents, doctors, or teachers. Younger children are often relegated to roles as pets or babies in the family (Schwartzman, 1978).

In general, the theories that have been available are not comprehensive but consider only selected elements in the play of young children. None of them, with the possible early exception of Isaacs (1933, 1930/1966), addresses the issue of play in the education of young children. However, some authors (Biber & Franklin, 1967; Fein & Rivkin, 1986; Forman & Hill, 1980; Kamii & DeVries, 1980) have recently attempted to provide bridges from selected theories to practice in the classroom.

CONCLUSION: THE NEED FOR RESEARCH

In reviewing the recent research on play from the perspective of the teacher, we have noted the abundance of material that has potential interest for teachers of young children. At the same time we have suggested that the available theory is not always clear. The different kinds of play are not always well defined. The functions they serve and the relationships among them are sometimes ambiguous.

Not all questions raised by teachers are "answerable" by reference to theory or research information. To answer their own questions teachers must often carry out their own research in their own settings. Much of this research is informal, as common as the "What if I tried this?" questioning that good teachers use both on the spot, to support learning, or in reflection over the day's activities.

What makes a "researchable question" one that facilitates change is the ability to step in and out of one's role as teacher/participant in the setting and alternate it with the role of observer of the entire picture. Understanding how what is observed is meaningful in the lives of children and in the practice of the teacher is the key to sifting through the observer's collection of information and finding the themes that are relevant to the situation.

Van Hoorn, whose research is described in Chapter 3, studied infants and toddlers and found very little information about play at that age level. She worked with the parents of these young children to discover what she needed to know. As you read Monighan-Nourot's account in Chapter 4, you will see that she observed that the youngest children in her setting, ages 2½ and 3, seemed distressed by admonitions to share. Thus the topic of sharing became the seed for her study examining the developmental functions of solitary play.

Comparing notes with other teachers and finding access to research grounded in teaching practice are other ways of bridging the participant/observer gap in one's own setting. Sometimes simply reading about or listening to someone else's experience sparks a researchable question that leads to change. Scales's account in Chapter 5 shows how, in discussing the work of researchers within her setting, she discovered that the presence of a teacher altered the character of spontaneous play. Consequently, Scales and her staff began to consider how they might monitor play events more sensitively.

Teachers have always shared their perspectives on play with others in informal ways such as in discussions in teachers' rooms, during staff meetings, and over potluck dinners. Unfortunately, valuable insights and important questions generated by this day-to-day informal research are seldom communicated to the broader audience of teachers. Moreover, just as teachers have little access to the work of researchers, researchers find little access to the teacher's daily experience.

The work of Van Hoorn, Monighan-Nourot, and Scales in the next three chapters forms bridges from educational practice to research. These early childhood educators dealt with the questions that arose over a period of several years in their individual work settings. During this time each of them became intrigued with a particular issue and looked at the research to find out whether related questions had been explored. Based upon their reading and their own observations, they began informally to research the questions they were asking about play. Excited by the discoveries made in their initial research, each went on to do a more comprehensive and formal study, attempting to unite the intuition built upon years of practice with the more formal methods of researchers. Their accounts describe their journeys from the domain of the practitioner to the domain of the researcher, and the emergence of their growing understanding of children's play.

Common threads weave through the three stories, their genesis in practice, and the resolution of questions that contributed meaningfully to change. Important threads include

>The need for teachers to protect the experience of childhood and support play in educational settings
>A shared belief in the value of developmental theory in informing excellence in teaching
>A shared commitment to asking questions and seeking answers that lead to both understanding and change in the lives of children and their teachers

In addition to the common beliefs woven through their accounts, there were other similarities in the way they carried out their studies. Each teacher generated her research questions from authentic situations. Each looked at the research literature to find out whether related questions had been explored. All of these studies used multiple research approaches to collect information. One shared research approach was the naturalistic observation of play of children in the home or school. Finally, all the research had practical applications. All used the information they gathered from their research to effect change in the settings that had generated their questions.

Although the contexts, participants, and specifics of each project differ, the reader will find common themes that strike notes of familiarity. However, as teachers, you will want to interpret these findings and their relevance in the light of the needs of your own settings. Perhaps you will find inspiration for systematically seeking evidence that will answer some of your own questions.

3
games that babies
and mothers play

BY JUDITH VAN HOORN

"Here's a 'Loteria' game that we used to play in Mexico."
"I just can't find any more good books in Spanish."
"Look at these flimsy Mexican-style skirts for $18.00; I could make
a better one for less than $5.00."
"Why don't we make some books too — like we did last year?"

How often our Head Start staff-parent purchasing meetings ended on
this same note. Like many preschool programs, we seemed to discover
each year that our favorite materials were those that we made
ourselves. Others might view making our own materials as
"reinventing the wheel." We saw our products as "customized wheels"
that made our program run better.

As education coordinator, it was my responsibility to work with
staff and parents to develop a comprehensive educational program for
over 500 children and their families. We wanted the program to reflect
the diverse cultures of the area and the families — Hispanics, Anglos,
blacks, Asians — living in both rural and urban areas in San Joaquin
County, California. As I retrace the steps that led from developing
classroom curricula for preschool children to research on the games
that infants and mothers play, I find that my journey begins and ends
with attempts to meet the needs of children and families from different
cultures.

That particular year, staff and parents collected traditional
stories and made books with photographs showing local families
engaged in everyday activities. Parents brought in sewing machines

and cooperated to make culturally traditional clothes such as Mexican skirts for pretend play. Teachers in the more rural areas brought familiar materials from local stores — fieldworker hats and cherry picking baskets.

About that time, the national Head Start organization began a home-based program. Staff members called "home visitors" went into the homes of more than 75 preschool children in our area, focusing on the parents as the "primary educators of their child." Compared to the educational materials available for center-based programs, there were even fewer materials available for parents, particularly those that reflected different cultures. Many commercial parent-education materials appeared to be produced for middle-class Anglo families, even when the pictures portrayed blacks or Hispanics. Speaking as a former parent in the program as well as a home visitor, Josie repeated a common theme when she said, "My family from Mexico just wouldn't do things this way. We've got to try something else."

Again, parent groups and staff worked together to develop the curriculum. The home visitors, half of whom were former Head Start parents, identified many activities and practices that could be incorporated. Home visitors found that they had better results and better rapport with families when they started with an activity that the parent and child already did together, such as an everyday household task like sorting socks. They could begin by letting parents know that sharing such activities with the child was a good idea. Visitors and parents could then consider how the activity fostered the child's development. They could vary or extend the activity in developmentally appropriate ways, such as cutting out pictures of clothes from a catalog and sorting the pictures. Within the context of the familiar, the visitor used a family routine to suggest new but related ideas.

It soon became apparent that, for the curriculum to reflect the culture of the families, we needed more information on each culture. How did families from different cultures understand the child-rearing process? What child-rearing practices did they use? What were their goals for their children?

In addition to a growing interest in culture, we also had a growing interest in play. Staff members noted that many of the most successful activities — those that were both educational and mutually enjoyable — drew upon what parents often called "just play." Home visitors observed that, when some parents tried to teach an activity to their children, they would adopt a "strict or punitive teacher" mode of interaction. For example, when teaching colors some parents first drilled, then grilled their children on five or six new words. On the other hand, when those same parents played with children for mutual enjoyment, they provided emotional support and social responsiveness, in addition to physical, cognitive, or linguistic challenges. For example, parents and children enjoyed taking turns when playing the game "I see something (red) — do you?"

Our dual interest in play and in culture led to discussions about play from a multicultural perspective? What do people from a given culture call "play"? Are young children encouraged to play? When? Who plays with the children? How?

My initial research foray in the area of infant play also developed out of questions that the home visitors asked: "What should we do with the babies in the homes?" Head Start teachers had always welcomed infants and toddlers into the classroom, but their visits had been temporary. In the home-based program however, they were permanent members, present — and often active and vocal — during each home visit. In addition to the focal, preschool child, the home visitor was supposed to help parents meet the needs of all the children in the home. Parents asked the most questions about infants, and visitors tried to provide the information they requested.

Meanwhile, research on infant development began to flourish and the demand for daycare expanded steadily. Popular books on infant development such as Brazelton's *Toddlers and Parents* (1974) appeared. "If we could only have a home-based program that focused on infants" was a refrain that each of us repeated more often as the years went by.

From the start of the home-based program, home visitors and parents often played traditional "baby games" to distract the infant while the "real work" of the visit was accomplished. As we recognized the importance of looking at development from infancy, the games themselves became important. Here was an activity the parents already did that was obviously fun for both parent and infant. We began to discuss the social, cultural, physical, and intellectual dimensions of the games. For example, pat-a-cake, known to all the U.S.-born staff and parents, involved clapping and making correspondences among word, meaning, and action. Parents and staff from different cultures also had their own repertoire of games.

PRELIMINARY RESEARCH

Knowing that Head Start was considering the possible expansion downward to include infants, I took my first course in infant development and opted to do research to answer some of the questions we were raising. Little did I know then that this would take me beyond the literature of infant development to that of play and games and of cultural differences among children.

fieldwork

I anticipated a small study in which I would observe games played by infants and parents of different cultural backgrounds. I did not envision the larger study, involving 152 parents from four different cultures, that grew from the first. Nor did I foresee that focusing on games in the home setting would be such an effective way of sharing with and learning from parents.

The purpose of this initial study was to collect games, to analyze them, and to find out about the games that others in child development and related fields had collected and written about. I decided to study the four largest ethnic groups in the program: Mexicans, Filipinos, Chinese, and U.S. Americans of European descent.

In collecting the games, I informally interviewed 5 to 10 parents and grandparents from each ethnic group. Even with this small sample, I collected a total of more than 30 different games representing all four cultures. These traditional infant games involved the very behaviors that were emphasized in parenting programs, such as physical closeness, talking to infants, and physical stimulation. For example, when playing the U.S. American game pat-a-cake, parents place the infant close to them and repeat a jingle while maintaining eye contact with the infant. They usually hold the infant's hands and lead the infant in a series of hand gestures that accompany the words. The game ends with smiles and affectionate squeezes. In effect, the games matched the goals of the Head Start home-based program. They appeared to be culturally developed and "field-tested" parenting programs. And they were free! I prepared a summary booklet from this informal research, including the text and description of each game as well as suggestions of how the games might be used.

researching available literature

During this preliminary research, I began to review the research literature. I thought that there would be many similar collections and analyses. Surprisingly, there were only a few analyses of infant games (e.g., Bruner, 1976; Call & Marschak, 1966). No collection was as extensive as mine. At this point, I began to consider a more comprehensive study. In addition to extending the number of participants, I wished to observe the way in which parents and infants played as well as to interview parents. Certain issues needed to be clarified, however, before undertaking a larger study. These included

1. How could the concept of "games" be defined?
2. How do games promote infant development?
3. How do games reflect various cultural child-rearing values?
4. What more do I need to know about the cultures I am studying?

DEFINING GAMES. My question was, What is an infant game? Parents and staff alike called these activities "games." Were they games to researchers as well? The literature indicated that, just as play has been observed among people of all ages in most cultures, so have games. And, just as it has been difficult for writers to frame a definition for play, defining "a game" has also proved difficult. Almost all definitions emphasize that, in addition to having the features of play, games have set rules and involve competition (Avedon & Sutton-Smith, 1971; Opie & Opie, 1976; Roberts, Arth, & Bush, 1959). For Avedon and Sutton-Smith (1971) this is explicitly true for infant games as well as games for children and adults. For example, when a baby finally succeeds in grasping the mother's fingers, "we speak of a goal being achieved and . . . a winner" (p. 7).

Others have challenged the notion that competition is a basic feature of all games. Schwartzman (1978) writes that competition may not characterize games in all societies, particularly those in which it is not valued. The activities collected in my preliminary research did not appear competitive. Was this generally true of all the activities parents called infant games? If I collected all the activities that parents themselves considered "games," I could then analyze them to determine their common features.

PROMOTING INFANT DEVELOPMENT THROUGH GAMES. The second issue that grew out of the initial research was the function of games. Parents, staff members, and the Head Start program wanted to *promote* children's development. If infant games were indeed "culturally developed parenting programs," games should foster infants' development. Was there support in the literature for viewing infant play, and in particular infant games, as a way to enhance development?

Substantial literature supports the importance of play for the infant's social development (Beckwith, 1985). Early play promotes bonding. Stern (1977) notes that, in play, both parent and infant participate in creating activity that both enjoy. Physical activity is an obvious feature of most infant games; however, no studies were found that focused on physical development.

In describing infants' cognitive development, Piaget (1954) used examples from his observations of his own three children that are strikingly similar to the parent-child interaction I observed in infant games. For example, in his description of the development of object permanence, Piaget included a playful episode involving his daughter, Jacqueline, then aged 10 months. When he took her toy parrot and hid it under her mattress to her left, she quickly found it. When he then hid it under the mattress to her right, Jacqueline continued to search on the left side where she had originally found it. This example is similar to games such as peek-a-boo and hide-and-seek, in which the partner disappears and reappears.

Piaget describes six substages in the development of object permanence. This raised questions about the timing of the games. Do parents introduce a game with a particular feature such as object permanence at the time when the infant is developmentally able to take part? Do parents modify the games to make them more cognitively challenging as the infant progresses from one substage to the next?

Piaget also described six parallel substages in the development of imitation, pretense, and physical causality. Some of the games collected in my initial research also involved imitation, pretense, and physical causality. So, these six stages Piaget described could be used for an analysis of these cognitive features of infant games.

SEEING GAMES AS REFLECTIONS OF CULTURAL VALUES. Anthropologists as well as developmental psychologists who have studied people from different cultures relate child-rearing practices to cultural differences (e.g., Erikson, 1950; Hsu, 1970; Mead, 1951; Parish & Whyte, 1978; Whiting, 1963). Accordingly, one would expect that the games and the manner in which they were played would differ among the four cultures in the study. The literature on games and culture supported this hypothesis.

The most extensive work on games and culture has been done by Sutton-Smith and Roberts, together and with other colleagues. They relate the features of games to characteristics of the society and to the child-rearing process. For example, games of strategy such as chess are related both to the social complexity in the society (Roberts et al.,

1959) and to stricter obedience training (Roberts & Sutton-Smith, 1962).

Burridge (1976) also describes ways that games reflect cultural values. Equality is an important aspect of Tangu relationships, and the idea of equality is central to the popular Tangu game "Taketak." As children play this game, they learn that everyone should have equal shares.

Eifermann's (1970) study of the games of kibbutz children provides the most detailed evidence for the relationship between a particular culture and children's games. The Israeli kibbutz contrasts with the nonkibbutz setting in that its child-rearing environment has been consciously developed by adults in order to instill certain values such as cooperation and placing the collective needs of the kibbutz above one's individual needs. Eifermann found that the kibbutz's values were expressed in the children's games. Unlike Israeli children from other environments, kibbutz children play cooperative group games almost exclusively.

This literature on games and culture gave further support to the hypothesis that parent-infant games from different cultures would differ and that the differences would reflect the culture. Viewed in this light, games function to enculturate infants to the culture of their parents. Games enhance universal developmental skills in culturally appropriate ways. Games also help infants develop values or skills that might be unique to a particular culture. If these hypotheses could be supported, they would provide additional rationale for including games as part of the curriculum.

LEARNING MORE ABOUT DIFFERENT CULTURES. To relate the features of the games to the cultures of the families in the study, I needed to find out a great deal more about the cultures. More reading about each group and conversations with its members yielded more information about its history, traditions, values, and cultural practices. Unfortunately, the literature offered little information on child-rearing practices, but it generally supported and explained my informal observations and helped me formulate questions for the research.

For example, according to the literature on Chinese values and customs, the measure of life is in family relationships (Wolf, 1968). The sense of self is the sense of being an integral part of the whole, the family, rather than the sense of being an isolated individual (Hsu, 1970). The world of children and adults is not separated; parents take children wherever they go. Children are subject to the authority of many older persons who help the child become integrated into the family and the community. How do Chinese infant games reflect these traditions? Would texts of the games refer to family life? Would many relatives play the games with the baby?

The literature on Filipino culture emphasized the effects of its many-faceted heritage on the Filipino people (Cordero & Panopia, 1976). Individual differences are tolerated. Harmony in personal relationships is valued. Polite language, a gentle voice, and hospitality are important behaviors. Would Filipino infant games reflect this diverse heritage or emphasize smooth personal relationships?

The information on U.S. culture and child-rearing practices provided a contrast to the information on Filipinos. Again, statements in the literature were consistent with many of my own observations. Among the early colonists of the United States, individual strength and perseverance were essential for survival; therefore, independence became a valued personality trait (Hsu, 1970). The American ideal is that all individuals can achieve their goal through their own hard work, individual talent, and ability to compete (Minturn & Lambert, 1964). Child-rearing practices reflect these cultural values. Independence training begins shortly after birth, when infants are put to sleep in their own rooms and often allowed to "cry it out." Achievement is emphasized and children are compared in order to see who is superior (Fischer & Fischer, 1963). Based upon this anthropological literature it seemed that the games that U.S. American parents would play with their infants might be much more competitive than those played by Chinese or Filipino parents.

In contrast to the literature on Chinese, Filipino, and U.S. American culture, the literature about Mexican culture portrayed people who were very different from the people I knew. For example, Ramos, a Mexican social philosopher, writes that "each individual lives closed within himself like an oyster within its shell" (Ramos, 1962, p. 72). Both Mexican writers and U.S. American trained anthropologists often focused on similar aspects of the Mexican Mestizo personality (Foster, 1979; Kearney, 1972; Pi-Sunyer, 1973; Ramos, 1962). The writers whose work was reviewed describe primarily the Mexican male. The lives of women are only briefly mentioned; the lives of children rarely. The discrepancy between the culture I have observed and that described in the literature suggests that researchers need to be wary of drawing generalizations from literature that may not be applicable to the subgroup they are studying.

PLANNING THE LARGER RESEARCH PROJECT

posing the questions

My preliminary study had raised many questions that were important not only from the viewpoint of researchers but also from our viewpoint as practitioners. Which were the most important for our purposes? If we planned to include infant games in the parent-education program, the first question was, What do we mean by "infant games"? To answer this we would have to examine the characteristics of the games. Based upon the literature, I hypothesized that the features of infant games would differ from culture to culture. This raised a second question, What is the relationship between the characteristics of the game and the culture of the family?

In my preliminary report, I had discussed ways in which infant games might foster development. Because our program emphasized cognitive development, I decided to limit the larger study to several specific aspects of cognitive development described by Piaget: pretense, imitation, object permanence, and causality. The games could be used to foster development in these areas if parents introduced them at developmentally appropriate times and then modified them to make them more challenging as the infant's cognitive abilities developed. Timing was critical. The third question I posed, therefore, was, What evidence could I find about the ways parents introduce and modify games, in order to promote cognitive development?

setting up the fieldwork

The anthropological and psychological literature on child-rearing practices in the four cultures used in my earlier study was also helpful in suggesting the methods to be used in the subsequent study. Anthropologists study people in their own environment and observe what people do as well as listen to what they say they do. They try to develop close relationships with their informants, in order to gain insight into how people from within a culture understand their own values and customs. This is called an *emic* perspective, in contrast to an *etic* perspective, which is the perspective of the outsider who studies the culture as an objective phenomenon. In addition to asking the parents for their own interpretations (emic perspective) of games, I decided to conduct the interviews and observations in participants' homes in order to assure that the setting was familiar and the interactions as typical as possible.

I drew upon the psychological literature on in-home studies of infants as I developed the written schedules for questioning the parents. The final interview schedule had two parts. In the first, participants were asked to describe each of the games they currently played with their infants. (A separate form was used for each game.) The second part was designed to obtain additional information about the context in which the games were played. Some of the information focused on the developmental level of the infant, for example, "Can your baby turn over?" Demographic items included family members' birthplace, age, years in the United States, education, and occupation. Key items elicited information regarding childcare patterns in the home, for example, "Who feeds . . . plays with . . . diapers the baby?" Lastly, items related to culture were included, such as, "Tell me about how (Chinese) raise their children? How do they play with them? What do most (Chinese) think are the qualities of a good (Chinese)?"

After completing the interview, participants were asked to demonstrate the games. The observation schedule for this included contextual information (e.g., a list of the people present) and a written record of both the text of the game and behavior of the participants. A second section included items needed for an analysis of the game with respect to interactive patterns (tempo, style, mood) as well as evidence of pretense, imitation, rules, and causality.

After developing the interview and observation schedules, I tried them out in several homes with English-speaking families from each culture. Based on these visits, some items were changed, added, or omitted. An initial, unstructured introduction for establishing rapport with the family and infant was added. As a final dress rehearsal, and in order to make sure that the data gathered were reliable, a colleague and I conducted interviews and observations of two families and compared our records. Since we agreed on 80% of the observations and 90% of the interviews, I could assume that my notes were not idiosyncratic and that someone else with similar training would include basically the same information.

These preliminary visits showed that it was difficult to arrange a time at which both parents would be at home. I was then faced with the difficult decision of whether to limit the sample to mothers in order to have a bigger sample, or to include both parents and have a smaller sample of families. I reluctantly decided to limit the study to mothers in order to include more infants.

To assist in the interviews and observations, I found and trained three assistants who were local teachers and each an immigrant — one Chinese, one Filipino, and one Mexican.

The most time-consuming and exhausting part of this stage of the research was finding the participants. I had decided to limit the age of the infants from 1 to 18 months and to include at least 20 families from each group. The easily available Head Start population had too few immigrant parents and infants in this age range. My assistants solved this problem by suggesting that we contact additional participants through referrals from organizations, educational providers, medical providers, and neighborhood churches. A list of infants and their parents was prepared from county birth records and shown to people from these organizations so they could identify any families they personally knew. We despaired when we saw that the Chinese group was relatively small. Birth records showed only 30 infants of appropriate age whose parents were both born in China or Hong Kong. Would 20 mothers agree to participate?

Fortunately, more than 90% of all those we reached through phone calls or visits agreed to take part in the study. The total sample included 20 immigrant mothers from China, 37 from the Philippines, and 47 from Mexico, plus 48 U.S. American mothers of European descent.

CARRYING OUT THE LARGER
RESEARCH PROJECT

a typical visit

No two visits were the same. There were mothers with small families and large families, older infants and younger infants. There were outgoing mothers and shy mothers. There were mothers who worked 12 hours a day picking cherries and came home to cramped quarters to fix dinners for families of seven; there were mothers who didn't work outside of the home and had one infant to care for. Nevertheless, a definite pattern, structured by the research procedure, typified most visits.

Let's look in detail at our visit with a 26-year-old mother from China, Mrs. T, whose daughter Jenny is 12 months old. When we arrive at Mrs. T's house she greets us at the door and leads us into the family room, a room with Western-style furniture and some Chinese decorations such as statues and scrolls. She introduces her 60-year-old "grandma," her 2½-year-old son, and Jenny. As the Chinese assistant greets the grandmother in Toisonese, their common native dialect, Mrs. T goes into the kitchen and reappears with iced tea, fruit, salted Chinese-style dried plums, and some almond cookies. She and the assistant exchange news about mutual friends in Toisonese. Mrs. T's grandmother does not understand English and I do not understand Toisonese, so the conversation flows back and forth from English to Toisonese. The assistant explains to Mrs. T that the purpose of the research is to find out how parents from different cultures play with their infants. She asks Mrs. T to describe and demonstrate games that she now plays with Jenny. Mrs. T begins by saying that she only plays games in Chinese. She then describes and demonstrates the four games she currently plays.

The first, called "Count the Insects" (see Figure 1), is one that she learned from her grandmother when she was growing up in Hong Kong. She thinks that most Chinese know this game. When asked about the purpose of the game, she explains that it helps Jenny improve her eye-hand coordination and learn body parts.

To demonstrate this game, Mrs. T places Jenny on the table facing her, holding Jenny's hand in a fist with only the index finger pointing. She points Jenny's index fingers together several times and says, in Chinese,* "Count the insects." She opens Jenny's arms wider and waves the index finger outward and inward, saying, "Insects fly, fly, fly, fly." Finally, she waves one finger in front of Jenny's nose and says,

Figure 1
"Count the Insects"

點 蟲 蟲　　　　Dim chùng-chúng.
　　　　　　　　See the insects.

蟲 蟲 飛　　　　Chùng-Chúng fei.
　　　　　　　　Insects fly.

飛 到 ……的 鼻　Fei deu Jenny ge beih.
　　　　　　　　Fly to Jenny's nose.

---

*Note that most descriptions of games in this chapter give English translations of rhymes, phrases, and dialogue that actually occurred in the speaker's native dialect.

"Fly to the top of Jenny's nose." Mrs. T ends the game by holding Jenny's hand and tickling her belly button with it. A few minutes later, as the adults talk, Jenny walks nearby, claps her hands, and points her index fingers together.

The second game Mrs. T demonstrates is a tickling game she learned from an uncle who manages a factory in Kwangtung Province. She lays Jenny on the carpet while she kneels above her. When Mrs. T blows on her stomach, Jenny laughs, squirms, and smiles. Next Mrs. T tickles her armpit, then her chest, abdomen, and neck while saying, "Chica, chica, chica" (nonsense sounds).

Mrs. T describes the third game as a clapping game, another one that she learned from her grandmother when she was a young child. She thinks most Chinese also know it. In this game she holds and claps Jenny's hands while reciting a rhyme in Chinese that begins "Clap your hand. Trade a banana. If the banana is sweet, trade it for a sickle."

The last game Mrs. T demonstrates is one she refers to as a "swinging game." She says that she made it up when her 2½-year-old son was an infant. She plays it "to train Jenny to be less fearful." Mrs. T picks Jenny up and kisses her. Then, still kissing her, she swings her around. She stops, looks into Jenny's eyes, and then swings around several more times. When her son comes over to watch, she puts the baby down and swings him. By this time all three look slightly dizzy. Her son staggers a bit and laughs and we all join him.

After we have something to eat, Grandma talks to the children while the assistant completes the last part of the interview that deals with demographic and child-rearing information. Mrs. T tells us that she is 26, completed 2 years of college in Hong Kong, and came to the United States 6 years ago. She is a homemaker. She and her husband were both born in Hong Kong. Her grandmother lives with them. Her father, mother, and brothers also live in the same town. Her husband, 32 years old, completed 4 years of college in Hong Kong before coming to the United States 8 years ago. He works as a chemist. At home, she and her husband speak Cantonese, Toisonese, and English. They speak to the children in all three languages. Her grandmother speaks to the children in Toisonese.

Describing Chinese values, Mrs. T says that Chinese people believe that a good Chinese is intelligent, knows how to conduct himself or herself properly, has leadership qualities, and is a hard worker. People help their children grow up to have these qualities "by telling them" and by example. When asked what kind of person she would like to see Jenny become at age 20, Mrs. T replies, "healthy, a good listener, a good student in college, cooperative, and helpful."

Describing traditional child-rearing patterns, Mrs. T says that, according to Chinese custom, the mother and grandmother take care of the baby. In her own family, her husband and son also participate. Everyone in the family frequently plays with Jenny and generally assures that she is comfortable and safe. Mrs. T's grandmother feeds her more often than anyone else. Mrs. T and grandmother diaper Jenny more often than Mr. T. In contrast to these caretaking activities everyone often plays with her.

When asked how Jenny's life would be different if her family were back in Hong Kong, Mrs. T replies that Jenny would have a "poor atmosphere, not that much room to play, . . . food that was not as nutritious." In other respects, she emphasizes that she is bringing up Jenny in much the same way she would if she still lived in Hong Kong.

the games

The interview with Mrs. T was one of 20 conducted with Chinese mothers and one of a total of 152 interviews we completed. The games Mrs. T played were 4 of 450 games the mothers described or demonstrated. Some were games that only one mother played, but most were games played by at least three or four mothers from the same culture.

CHINESE GAMES. Three of the infant games Mrs. T played were played by several other mothers. Five demonstrated the "Count the Insects" game; three played the "Sickle" clapping game; and four others played similar swinging games. Another popular game was a rowing game in which the mother places the infant on her lap and they "row" back and forth in synchrony. The text of the game describes a good baby and happy grandmother: "Grandmother says I am a good baby. . . . Beats the drum and gong merrily, to accompany me home."

FILIPINO GAMES. Mrs. F holds her 7-month-old daughter, Lisa, facing her on her lap. She says "close-open" slowly and distinctly while she demonstrates by opening and closing her own right hand. Lisa looks intently at her mother, alternatively at her face and her hand. Mrs. F then picks up Lisa's right wrist. As she repeats "close-open," she gently closes Lisa's fingers to form a fist, then opens them again. Almost all Filipino mothers knew this ritualized game, "Close-Open." Perhaps it was the prototype game for them, for, when asked to tell about games they currently played, many responded, "Games like 'Close-Open?'"

Sixteen Filipino mothers played tickling games with their infants (2–18 months). Mothers wiggled their fingers to tickle the infant's stomach, chest, neck, cheeks, toes, lips, and armpits, or they nuzzled or kissed the infant's stomach or neck. Mothers sometimes accompanied tickling with vocalizations such as "hello baby . . . yee . . . ch . . . ch . . . ch . . . " or "kiliti-kiliti."

Mrs. P played another tickle game with her 18-month-old son Peter, while her older daughter Linda watched and smiled. This was one of the few games collected in a Filipino dialect rather than in English.

> Banog-Banog sa Cagon   Kite, kite of Cagon,
> *(Mrs. P moves hands "like a bird," starting high above Peter and "flying" downward.)*
>
> Asa motagdon   Where will it alight?
> *(Mrs. P's hands get lower and lower. Mrs. P's voice becomes more dramatic.)*
>
> Dinhi-Dinhi   Here. Here.
> *(Mrs. P suddenly brings her hands down to Peter's chest and tickles him. Mrs. P, Peter, and Linda all laugh.)*

MEXICAN GAMES. The most popular game was a clapping game, "Tortillitas," with a text about making little tortillas. Many versions were collected; the most common variation was:

> Tortillitas para mama,   Little tortillas for mom,
> Tortillitas para papa,   Little tortillas for dad,
> Las quemaditas para papa.   The little burned ones for dad.

Forty Mexican mothers played games that involved clapping, tickling, rocking, or swinging. Most games included rhymed verses. The following game, "Riqui Ran," was played by 10 mothers with infants 1 to 8 months old. It is striking for the energetic rocking of the infant's torso and is often played as follows. Mrs. C sits with Miguel on her lap, facing her. She rocks both of them forward and backward until the last line. On the last line she stops rocking and dramatically tickles Miguel under the chin.

> Riqui ran los maderos   Riqui ran, the carpenters
>   de San Juan   of San Juan
> Piden pan no les dan   They asked for bread and they
> Piden queso les dan hueso   don't give them any.

y se les atora en el	They ask for cheese. They

<table>
<tr><td>y se les atora en el
    pescuezo
y se ponen a llorar en la
    puerta del saguan.</td><td>They ask for cheese. They
    give them a bone
and it gets stuck in
    the throat
and they start to cry at
    the gate.</td></tr>
</table>

U.S. AMERICAN GAMES. Games of disappearance and reappearance were the most popular with U.S. American mothers. Peek-a-boo was played by 30 mothers with infants 2 to 18 months old. This game usually involved covering and uncovering either partner. The following version was played by Mrs. S and her 10-month-old daughter, Amber.

"Where did Amber go?" *(Mrs. S covers Amber's head with a cloth.)*
"There she is!"*(Amber uncovers herself. Mrs. S and Amber look*
    at each other; both smile.)
"Where's Amber?" *(Amber covers her own head.)*
"There she is!"*(Amber uncovers herself. Mrs. S and Amber look*
    at each other again; both smile.)

Four mothers with infants 13 to 18 months old played hide-and-seek as well as peek-a-boo. In hide-and seek, one partner disappears from the other's view and waits to be found.

The second most popular game was pat-a-cake, a sequenced game with clapping and other hand gestures. Mothers with young infants clap the infant's hands. Older infants sometimes clap their hands but are assisted with the other gestures.

(Mrs. C and 9-month-old daughter, Jessica, sit on the couch
    facing each other.)
"Pat-a-cake, pat-a-cake,
 Baker's man,
 Bake me a cake as fast as you can."
    (Mrs. C holds Jessica's hands and claps them together.)
"Pat it and roll it"
    (Mrs. C rolls Jessica's hands.)
"and mark it with a B"
    (Mrs. C writes "B" in the air.)
"and put it in the oven for baby and me!"
    (Mrs. C claps rhythm.)

researcher's interpretation

In a 6-month period of intense activity we visited the homes of 152 families. I conducted or assisted with more than 130 of these visits.

Each evening I reviewed the interview and observation schedules completed that day. Each day, as we drove from house to house, the research assistants and I discussed our observations. In addition, we met as a group to try to summarize what we were learning about the characteristics of infant games, the relationship between the games and the culture of the families, and our observations related to the four aspects of cognitive development.

As the weeks went by, we were particularly struck by the similarities across cultures regarding the features of the games. This was surprising because, based on the literature, I had expected to find major differences. It was surprising to the research assistants because they generally saw their own customs as being quite different from others'.

Driving on dusty country roads in the 100° heat of August, I looked forward to sitting in air-conditioned splendor, analyzing the data and drinking iced tea, and seeing the overall picture emerge. The pace of the research became tiring. I had started the interviews in the spring, at the leisurely pace of three or four per week. This pace gained great momentum during the summer when the assistants were on their vacations. We did up to 20 interviews a week, including evening and weekend visits. However, when the last of the interviews was completed and the analysis begun, I missed the fun of being with the families and found that, associated with the visits, even hot dusty roads became fond memories.

Research on infant play had been a fortunate choice. In addition to the very high rate of participation, the mothers' enthusiasm about sharing what and how they played, and the warm welcome they gave us, made this research emotionally as well as intellectually satisfying.

MAKING SENSE OF WHAT WE FOUND

I began the analysis of what the mothers had described and demonstrated as "games" by examining the characteristics of the games of each culture. These characteristics included the actions and texts as well as the interactive style or manner in which the mother played the game. This analysis enabled me to describe infant games. I also considered the features of rules and competition in order to compare my definition with that of others. This was the first step in the broader analysis of the relationship between games and culture, and in the analysis of the relationship between the timing of the games and the cognitive development of the infant.

I had developed the interview and observation schedule in anticipation of this analysis. I constructed categories for various characteristics, such as tempo, style, modality, and relationship between text and action. Many of these categories included scales, such as, for tempo, fast-medium-slow, or increasing-decreasing. In order to determine whether the games that involved pretense, imitation, object permanence, or causality were introduced at developmentally appropriate times, I computed the correlation between the number of infants of a given age who played a game with a particular feature such as pretense. This was computed separately for each culture.

I was then ready to formulate some answers to the three questions I had posed in the planning stage of this research project.

what are the features of an "infant game?"

There were great similarities in the ways that mothers understood the term *game*, as well as in the games they played. The large majority (about 80%) of the games were traditional ones they had learned from relatives, generally parents or grandparents, and had heard called "games." These games always involved actions, usually accompanied by a text. The actions as well as the relationship between action and text were similar across cultures. The actions in the games were the same as those in the preliminary study — primarily clapping, swinging, rocking, running, "finger play," tickling, and appearance and disappearance.

To describe these actions and their relationship to the text, I used the categories I had constructed: games with single actions, games with repeated actions, games with nonsequenced multiple actions, games with sequenced nonlogical actions, and games with sequenced logical actions. Tickling the infant once under the chin is an example of a single-action game. Repeat this and it becomes a game with a repeated action. Mothers from all cultures played games with repeated actions involving swinging, clapping, and rocking. Mothers from all cultures also played games with multiple nonsequenced actions. An example of one would be a game in which the mother kisses the infant, then tickles, then tosses the infant into the air. On the subsequent round she repeats these behaviors, but changes the sequence. Each culture had games with sequences that did not change. Some were nonlogical. In the Chinese game, "Gourd," for example, there is no logical reason why eating a piece of chicken should follow pointing to the sky. In contrast, pat-a-cake follows the logical sequence of actions one uses in baking a cake.

In all four cultures, actions and texts of the games are related. All games with three or more nonlogical sequenced actions are accompanied by long, formal, ritualized texts. For example, in pat-a-cake, mothers act out the text "Pat it and roll it and mark it with a B." All of these were traditional games that the mothers said were passed down from their parents or relatives. It appears that mothers use the text as a cue for the behavior and its sequence; otherwise, it would be difficult to remember the long sequence of actions. In contrast to these traditional games, none of the games the mothers had made up themselves had a text as complex as the ones accompanying the traditional games. None had three or more nonlogical sequenced actions. In this way the traditional games provide infants with opportunities to hear the repetition of complex linguistic patterns and to learn a fairly long behavioral pattern.

The interactive style, the manner in which infant and mother play the game, was distinct from most nonplay behaviors. Mothers smiled more frequently and used exaggerated facial expressions such as widening their eyes and gazing intently at the infant. Mothers also used vocal signals. They generally raised their pitch and used great rhythmic emphasis. Researchers have noted that these behaviors help maintain infants' attention (Stern, 1977) and communicate playfulness (Bateson, 1976). The message that "this is play" appeared effective in reducing any ambiguity about the mother's intent. For example, after a round of the Mexican clapping game "Tortillitas," Mrs. G exclaimed, "Mmm, tortillitas," and nibbled on her daughter Rosa's hand. But instead of responding with terror at being bitten, Rosa squealed with laughter and reached her other hand to her mother's mouth.

Like the communication of "this is play," certain styles of tempo, rhythm, synchrony, body contact, body orientation, and eye contact characterized infant games across cultures. Mothers of all cultural groups frequently commented on the cultural differences they found in many typical adult interactions: "Americans talk slow" or "Filipinos are friendly." In contrast to these stylistic differences that characterize adult-adult interactions in different cultures, infant-mother games were characterized by the same moderate tempos, rhythmic emphases, and synchrony between partners. Typically, the rhythm of the text was both exaggerated and coordinated with the action. Synchrony was achieved primarily through the mother's efforts, as she moved the infant's body in time to the text or adjusted the tempo of the text to the infant's independent movements. For example, in the Mexican game "Riqui Ran," the textual rhythm is pronounced, even to a non–Spanish speaker. The mother rocks the infant's body back and forth in synchrony with her own movements.

The structure of the game, rather than the style of the individual, generally determined the distance between players as well as the presence or absence of body contact. Most games involved direct manipulation or touching of the infant's body. Despite the possibilities for assuming different orientations, most games described or observed involved the partners situated in a face-to-face position with their torsos also facing each other. Of the 450 games played by 139 participants, only 69 games played by 49 participants were characterized by other orientations. Of this number, only 15 mothers played a game in which the infant's torso was turned away throughout the entire game. In the others, partners changed orientation, such as by moving toward and then away from each other.

Sustained eye contact between participants also was a feature of almost all games played by participants. If an infant was not visually attentive, the mothers tended to use increased vocalizations, movement, and facial expressions to establish and maintain eye contact.

After reviewing the literature on games, I had wondered whether infant games would be characterized by the presence of rules and competition. Most games did have rules, in that they were played in the same way again and again. Despite variations in texts and some actions, most mothers followed the same format when playing the game. With infant games, the pattern — the ritualized, repeated behavior — is the rule.

Avedon and Sutton-Smith's (1971) hypothesis that all infant games have elements of competition was not supported in this study. Chasing games and games of disappearance and reappearance do have a structure that provides for competition. Do mothers and infants play these games in a competitive manner? The following examples illustrate typical behavior patterns.

> Jason is sitting several feet from his mother. She gets down on her hands and knees. They look at each other for a moment.
> Remaining in place, his mother makes a sudden lunging movement. Immediately, Jason begins to crawl away. She crawls after him, reaches him, grabs his feet, and dramatically turns him onto his back. He squeals with laughter. Then they both pause, gazing at each other. Jason then turns over and quickly crawls away. He turns back, looking at her, crawls, turns and looks, and pauses. His mother, however, has returned to the couch and her role as interviewee.

In infant games mothers "play" with the *concept* of competition. For example, mothers from each culture play chasing games in which they introduce two antithetical roles, the chaser and the chased, or the hider and the seeker. This, then, is the "contest." But it is only a mock contest. All mothers from all four cultures play with the same implicit rules: The chaser and the seeker will always win. If the mother is the chaser, she will permit the infant to move about with growing excitement, but she will always be successful in catching him. If the infant is the chaser, the mother may move about, allowing the infant's excitement to mount, but she will always allow the infant to be successful in catching her. This, then, is a "contest" with an outcome assured by the player of greater power.

But what of the infant? It appears that the outcome is assured for infants as well. From observations of the infants' reactions, the climax of the game is the reunion of infant and mother. In visual games like peek-a-boo, an infant's eyes often widen with delight when the mother reappears. In games in which one hides and the other actively searches, the reunion is joyously celebrated. The same is true of chasing games. The older child playing this game may want to win, may evidence disappointment at being caught, at being the "loser." For infants, however, the chase must result in capture for the game to end. Perhaps this is one reason for this implicit rule.

Is there a winner? In one game, the infant who was caught by his mother laughed and immediately attempted to play another round. In another game, the mother who was caught happily exclaimed, "You found me!" Several infants played both roles, switching back and forth from the chaser to the chased. Their obvious joy with either role showed that catching and being caught are both equally delightful pieces of the "game" pie.

how do games reflect the culture of the families?

In contrast to what I had expected, I found striking similarities among the games from the four cultures. The manner in which people from different cultures play infant games is similar. The age at which different types of games are introduced is similar. Across cultures mothers learn more games in their own infancy from their relatives. Mothers from different cultures give the same reasons for playing the games.

In some ways games do appear to reflect the specific culture. The most basic way that the games transmit the culture is that they transmit the language. With only one exception, all mothers played only games from their own heritage. This is surprising because so many of the mothers had lived in the United States for more than 5 years and spoke English fairly fluently.

Some other specific and interesting differences seem to reflect particular cultural patterns. More of the Chinese texts mentioned family relationships. Many Chinese mothers stressed that their husbands loved to play with the infants. Perhaps this attests to the importance of the family in Chinese culture, emphasized both in the literature and by the participants.

Many of the Filipino games were didactic and played in English (e.g., "Close-open"). Several Filipino mothers thought that their parents learned these games from American missionaries. This would be in keeping with the literature on Filipino culture that emphasizes the disruption of the native cultures by 300 years of contact with the Spanish, Japanese, and Americans. Few Filipino mothers knew games in native dialects with texts that were more than a few lines long. This contrasted with the larger collections of games in the native dialects from other countries.

More U.S. American mothers encouraged their infants to play independently than did mothers from any of the other cultures. This is consistent with the mothers' own statements of American values as well as descriptions of anthropologists (Fischer & Fischer, 1963; Hsu, 1970).

Several of the Mexican games evidenced the hardships of living: "Tortillitas for dad and mom who are tired." "The carpenters of San Juan, they ask for bread and they don't give them any." The Mexican families in the study were, as a group, poorer than any other group. Most were farmworkers. Such hardships do reflect their lives. It would be interesting to find out whether these games are played as widely among middle-class families and whether middle-class families use the same texts.

These examples illustrate that some games do reflect the culture of the families. There was little difference in the way that the mothers played the games and the actions of the games. The main difference was the language used and what was said. The text is understood by the mother but not by the infant; therefore, the relationship between games and culture is stronger for the mother than for the child. Perhaps these games are of greater interest to mothers because of their texts. The texts refer to family, to life's hardships, to the baby. Mothers who like the texts would be more likely to play them more often.

do games promote cognitive development?

According to Piagetian theory, development occurs as the result of the organism's interaction with the environment. Did the interactions of the games foster development? For example, is a game that includes imitation introduced when the infant is old enough to imitate the behaviors? Is a game of peek-a-boo changed as the infant's concept of object permanence develops? Theoretically, there are numerous ways that a game could be adapted to the infant's growing capabilities.

In fact, my analysis of when games were introduced and the changes the mothers reported making indicated that games were rarely adapted to changes in the infant's development. Games that involved the concept of object permanence were exceptions. Mothers introduced games such as peek-a-boo within the first few months and changed the style of the game as the infant grew older. In playing hide-and-seek with an 18-month-old, the mother might hide in another room and wait for the infant to find her. Most games, however, were played in a highly ritualized manner that precluded much action on the part of the infant. For example, many mothers introduced clapping games when the infants were too young to clap independently. Mothers held and clapped their infants' hands. But even when the infants clapped independently as they walked about the house, mothers held their hands and clapped them during the games.

INTEGRATING GAMES
INTO PARENT-EDUCATION CURRICULA

After analyzing the data, I attempted to step back and integrate these findings with the development of parent-education curricula. Perhaps the most important contribution of the research was the validation of the mothers' understanding of the games. The mothers believed that these games would support their infants' development. The following are some of their reasons for believing in the value of games:

"For sheer enjoyment . . . laughter . . . for baby to become familiar with family member." (Chinese mother)

"For fun . . . baby smiles and laughs . . . stops crying. . . . [It] socializes baby . . . you talk to them and they listen." (Filipino mother)

"For fun . . . it makes baby happy . . . baby learns how to attract parents' attention . . . it's exercise . . . he's learning to understand . . . you communicate with baby . . . [he] will listen and learn to identify voices." (Mexican mother)

"It's a magical feeling . . . [develops] social togetherness. She knows mother loves her. . . . She learns how to be a loving, affectionate person. [In playing peek-a-boo] she learns mother is still there." (American mother)

The mother's perspective — the emic perspective — was supported by my analyses of the characteristics of the games — the etic perspective. Games are characterized by behaviors that promote mutuality, cooperation, and attachment. When playing games, the mother's primary purpose is "mutual enjoyment." This contrasts with her behavior in routine care activities with specific goals such as feeding, diapering, and dressing her infant. When playing games, mothers' behaviors are the very ones that researchers have found elicit infant attentiveness and smiling, that is, face-to-face orientation, synchrony, and rhythmic emphasis.

Infant games are characterized by cooperation rather than competition in both style and structure. The infant learns that the personal relationship is of primary importance. Games are one means by which infants first learn to cooperate within the family.

Games contribute to the infant's attachment to others in the family. In many families, fathers and siblings infrequently helped feed, bathe, or diaper the infant; however, across the sample, everyone played with the infant and most included infant games as part of playing. According to some mothers, playing together is the primary way that the infant gets to know some of the family members.

Infant games are intergenerational rituals that appear to contribute to a feeling of closeness across several generations. Across cultures, mothers reported that they learned a majority of the games from their own parents or grandparents. They spoke of this with warm feelings. Many mothers reported going back to their relatives now, as parents, and relearning some of the games they half remembered. When the infants in this study become parents with infants of their own, they may also use the games as a way of forging loving links among generations.

The analysis of the data led to two conclusions that run counter to widely held beliefs. First, unlike other child-rearing practices, infant games from different cultures involve similar parent-child interactions. Second, unlike some other forms of play, traditional games may not be modified in ways that promote the particular aspects of cognitive development I studied. Because these conclusions contradict major assumptions of both practitioners and researchers, further research is necessary. It would be interesting to check on whether or not these conclusions apply to games played by parents who currently live in Mexico, China, and the Philippines, rather than immigrants from those countries.

I began with the premise that infant games are part of a culturally developed parenting program. From both an emic and an etic perspective, the games do appear to contribute to the social and affective development of the infant. Rather than enculturating infants to cultural specifics, infant games help foster a more universal process, that is, they "enspeciate." Infant games help infants become loving, cooperative human beings.

This is the main goal of most parenting programs. In these programs parents are often "taught" to hold and touch their infants, to maintain frequent eye contact. When playing these games, all mothers exhibit all of these behaviors. Furthermore, playing these games is not seen as a separate activity, but as one that occurs throughout the day. No equipment is needed — just two people. When playing games, there is no "other agenda" — just having fun and feeling a sense of closeness.

When games that babies and their families play are included in parenting programs, parents and parent educators can learn from each other. Parents are experts at these games and enjoy sharing them. Educators can assist parents in understanding more about child development by using games as concrete examples when they discuss principles of development. They can affirm what parents already do. Together, educators and parents and infants from all cultures can enjoy these rituals — our shared legacy from past generations of parents.

4
conversations with the
real and imagined

BY PATRICIA MONIGHAN-NOUROT

It is the autumn of 1978. I see it happening again. One of the 3-year-olds is loudly protesting attempts by an older child to appropriate some of his small wooden blocks. A participating parent intervenes. Her voice carries an edge of anger or perhaps frustration, just as mine would. "But Ronnie, in this school we share our toys." Ronnie seems unconvinced by her admonitions. He kicks apart the building and the arrangement of small animals he has constructed and retreats to the pillow in the corner, thumb in his mouth, head hanging in defeat. Later that morning, in our wrap-up session, I discuss the events of the day with the parents who serve as staff members. I struggle to convey to them that sometimes children need to play alone, sometimes they need *not* to share. They listen, somewhat skeptically, and I feel I am on shaky ground.

These events happened at the beginning of my first year as teacher-director of a parent-participation preschool in a small Northern California community. I had taught in early childhood programs for 9 years and felt challenged by the prospect of a multi-aged setting with younger children, aged 2½ to 5. As an elementary-school teacher, I found the developmental differences between kindergartners and first graders fascinating. Their bodies and minds changed a lot in one year. They moved more skillfully, progressing from the modest climbing structure to the parallel bars. As 6-year-olds they became skilled at negotiating taking turns with peers and told jokes with puns that revealed their understanding of our language system.

The pressure of the educational system to ignore these differences was a major reason I left the public schools. Block corners and dress-up clothes were being rapidly displaced by dittoes and craft projects exalting the "letter of the week" in the kindergartens of public schools. Pressure mounted to change many of my beliefs about teaching young children, beliefs that were based on my conviction that young children learn best through their play. When I was offered the opportunity to run my own preschool program, it seemed a safe haven. The world of imagination and exploration, of role play and trikes would remain sacred to the preschool teacher. And to their parents? I was to find reasons to wonder.

Another challenge to me was trying to understand the developmental differences I saw within my preschool group. Available curriculum books seemed to describe activities intended to be appropriate for "all preschool-aged children," and comments on their play were laced with platitudes such as "Play is the child's work." It seemed that there were powerful differences in the ways that younger and older children played at preschool.

My questions were more specific. I wanted to know *why* 3-year-olds seemed to want to play alone. How was it that fours and fives preferred poker chips or wooden beads to the plastic replicas of fried potatoes and fruit that were purchased? Was a child's conversation aloud to herself simply an indication of her inability to communicate, or did her behavior contribute to her growth?

FINDING OUT ABOUT IMAGINARY COMPANIONS

reviewing the literature

As these questions emerged from my observations in my own classroom, I sought answers in books describing development in early childhood. Most of the descriptions of children's play stressed the immaturity of solitary play for preschool children, and some included techniques for encouraging children to play cooperatively in groups. Group socialization appeared to be the implicit goal served by preschool play experience.

Further reading revealed that the most commonly expressed view of the role of solitary play was based on research conducted by Parten (1932). She traced the developmental sequence of preschool play from solitary to parallel to associative and cooperative play in the parent-participation preschool she studied. A more recent replication of her work by Barnes (1971) largely corroborated this sequence, although the older children engaged in more solitary play than Parten had reported.

The research literature also revealed information about children's play written from the psychoanalytic perspective. My own motivation for delving into this area came from the father of a child in my classroom, who expressed concern over his daughter's long conversations with an imaginary friend. He worried that her chances for academic success and social adjustment were undermined by her expeditions into fantasy. One study, by Ames and Learned (1946), supported my intuition that early childhood imaginary companions were both normal and healthy manifestations of developing imagination. Research conducted by Singer and Singer (1980) on the development of imagination bolstered my hunch that such imaginary friends might even contribute to later creative abilities. However, I failed to convince the child's father, who began to ridicule his daughter for her imaginary friend and asked for a referral to a competent child psychotherapist.

Partly to satisfy my own curiosity and partly to document the normality of imaginary friends for this parent, I did some research of my own. I developed questionnaires and distributed them to parents in my school, following up with additional questions during parent conferences. I asked the parents about their perceptions of their children's make-believe play at home. Later, in informal interviews with the children, I asked similar questions, following a format suggested by Singer (1973). Children and parents in this small study told me about the children's favorite play activities, the characteristics of their beloved stuffed animals, and the personalities of and experiences they had with their toys and/or imaginary playmates. The results were similar to those reported by Ames and Learned (1946): About 30% of the 24 children aged 2½ to 5 described imaginary friends. In most cases the parents were either actively supportive or said they "did not interfere" with their children's imaginary companions. This news eased the mind of the concerned father, who, comforted by evidence of his daughter's normal development, allowed the imaginary bunny back into the family.

Efforts to understand better the development of preschool children's play and how to support it in the classroom had also led me to the work of Smilansky (1968) who studied young children in Israel. She studied the complexity of role play created by children, using Piaget's categories (functional/sensorimotor; constructive; dramatic; games with rules) that are described in detail in Chapter 2. Smilansky expressed the provocative idea that adult intervention in children's play might foster the development of cognition and symbolic abstraction.

applying other researchers' categories to my own observations

The ground work had been set for me to look differently at the play of children in my classroom. In the past, 5-minute, hand-recorded anecdotal records of children's activity had served as a basis for parent conferences and developmental assessments. These revealed how characteristics of children's spontaneous play behavior changed over time and allowed me to maintain my view of the "whole child" as she or he developed. I found this perspective valuable amidst the proliferation of "draw a shape," "cut a line," "write your name" assessments popular as kindergarten readiness exercises.

From Smilansky's (1968) categories — functional, constructive, dramatic, and games with rules — I learned that play reflected children's increasing ability to use abstract elements in their play. Children use their capacity for mental representation and imagination to create make-believe symbols. Such "distance" from concrete objects and present time and space is thought to increase as children mature and gain experience in using abstract symbols to create meaning (Sigel, 1982). For example, the child who is able to pretend to drink milk from a block of wood reflects more symbolic "distance" in her play than the child who must have a toy cup in order to pretend. As children mature, imaginary objects and hypothetical situations gradually displace the need for concrete objects to support the use of imagination in pretend play.

Studies of social play (Barnes, 1971; Parten, 1932) described children's play in terms of their abilities to interact successfully with others. Solitary play was labeled as the most immature form, reflecting an inability to share materials and negotiate roles and themes with playmates. Parallel play — when children play in the same area or with the same materials, but with no interaction observed — was described as the next "level" of play. Group play included children's associating with one another in sharing objects and space (as in the block corner) and cooperating and negotiating over roles and play themes. This latter was assumed to be the most sophisticated form of play observed during the preschool years.

The research I had read allowed me to impose a more specifically defined developmental framework on my observations. It seemed

plausible to determine both the social and the symbolic sophistication of children by applying these ideas to my collection of
observations. First I "coded" my classroom observations according
to the level of cognitive "distance" evidenced, that is, for functional,
constructive, dramatic, or rule-based play. Then each observation
also was "coded" as solitary, parallel, or group play. A subsequent
analysis showed that the idea of increasing abstraction with age
"fit" the patterns of behavior in my classroom. For example, 3-year-
olds and 5-year-olds clearly differed in the degree of mental
representation they used in their play. Younger children were more
likely to construct a symbolic representation and end the play
sequence at that point.

> Daniel (3 years, 9 months) makes some holes with his index finger
> in the mound of playdough at his place. He says, "This is a big one.
> A big pizza. I'm dipping in big dots." He puts three candles in the
> holes, then adds a plastic candle holder.

Older preschool children integrated increasingly abstract elements
into their symbolic play, often "layering" a dramatic sequence onto a
concrete construction.

> Samantha (5 years, 2 months) plays alone in the block corner.
> "Oh, here's another one," she says to herself as she adds a block
> connecting two upright blocks. "There's the tower for the castle."
> She places two small blocks inside her structure. "The thrones for
> the King and Queen." Samantha begins to rock the "castle." "Oh
> no! It's an earthquake! A tornado!" She sweeps her arms over the
> blocks as the building collapses.

Examples like these partially explained why some children preferred
ambiguous or unstructured objects for their play: They had more
freedom to transform those objects and give full rein to their
imaginations.

But I had difficulty reconciling Parten's (1932) categories of social
play with what I observed in my classroom. Particularly discrepant
was the assumption that only the youngest children played alone.
Many of the sophisticated players of group fantasy at 4 or 5 years old
engaged in as much solitary play as the 2- and 3-year-olds in the
group. I began to consider Singer's (1973) ideas that privacy may play
a key role in the development of imagination skills. Could it be that the
older children chose to play alone sometimes in order to consolidate
their make-believe creations?

Further reading led me to research by Rubin, Watson, and Jambor (1978) on preschoolers' play. Their work also questioned the view that solitary play represented the most immature behavior for preschool children. As an alternative to looking at play in terms of cognitive complexity and social complexity separately, they nested the cognitive categories described by Smilansky (1968) within the social play and determined how sophisticated it was in terms of symbolic distancing. Solitary play, for example, might be functional in nature, as when a child pours sand repeatedly through a funnel and sings to herself as she plays. It might also contain elements of symbolism, as in a dramatic scenario played out with mother and baby animals in a toy farm. Rubin et al. noted that, in the setting they studied, children throughout the preschool years played alone; however, as they developed, the nature of that play became more intellectually sophisticated. Would this comparison hold true for my classroom? How could I determine when solitary play was normal adaptive behavior and when there was cause for concern that a child was withdrawing from her peers?

Watching children as they moved from solitary to group activity, I noted the differences in the way older children as compared to younger children showed when they wanted privacy or preferred to be social. A 5-year-old might typically remark, "I'm doing this now. I'll come to your restaurant later." In contrast, a 3-year-old might either physically fight intrusion on his solitary activity by grabbing objects and shouting "No! Mine!" or retreat from play as Ronnie had done.

Sometime during the preschool years, it seemed, children learned to communicate effectively their needs for private activity to others through language.

listening to language
from a developmental perspective

Reading the research on the development of language during the preschool years provided an important link in my understanding of how children shifted between social and private forms of play. I had carefully documented both solitary and group play in my classroom, as well as the kinds of props and roles children used in constructing their imaginative domains. Now my focus shifted to the means by which these imaginative constructions are maintained: language.

The developmental fate and function of what psychologists call "egocentric speech" seemed intriguing. Piaget (1969) describes such speech as one example of the kind of "egocentric thought" typical of young children. "Egocentric" implies a limitation on young children's ability to address or consider viewpoints other than their own in any given situation. A good example of this is the collective monologue teachers commonly observe in preschool classrooms. Here children appear to be engaged in social conversation. The content, however, is simply each child talking to himself, while taking turns typical of a dialogue or group conversation:

> HEIDI. I'm making potato chips. *(She places tiny pieces of play-dough along the edge of a wooden popsicle stick.)*
> JESSICA. *(As she massages a piece of playdough)* Alice is taking off her shoes.
> HEIDI. *(Picking up some birthday candle holders from the table)* Him drop these.
> JESSICA. She putted her other shoe on now.

Piaget (1969) describes the decline of egocentric thought and language as children develop as being a process whereby the view of self gradually expands in order to adapt to others. Vygotsky, a Russian contemporary of Piaget, also considered this idea. Vygotsky (1962) saw "private" speech as a separate kind of communication that develops during early childhood. As young children, we learn to communicate both with ourselves and with others; however, until the age of 6 or 7, both kinds of communication, private and social, are spoken aloud. As children's mental capacity grows, communication with the self begins to take place silently as conversations about real and imagined experience become what adults call recollection and fantasy.

I became interested in how this process of "thinking aloud," so common in young children, changed as they approached school age and began to differentiate private and social activities. Were these changes in spoken language related to the changes observed in the social and cognitive complexity of play? How were solitary play and private speech connected? Did parallel play and collective monologue occur together? How did social speech and cooperative group play relate to one another? And, finally, how could I use observations of both language and play to focus on the developmental differences in my multi-aged preschool group?

LOOKING AT LANGUAGE AND PLAY:
A SMALL STUDY

In setting up a study, I started out with a small sample of 12 children, divided into three age groups with two boys and two girls in each.

Group I children were 2½ to 3½ years old; Group II were 3½ to 4½; and Group III were 4½ to 5½. Over a period of 6 weeks, three 5-minute observations were collected on each child, for a total of 15 minutes. Initially, I videotaped children during the free play period in the classroom, but I found the video tapes difficult to analyze for private speech, which is often spoken in a low tone and quietly. The videotape microphones did not record many of these softly spoken sounds, and it was difficult to determine what children were saying. Hand-recorded observations seemed less intrusive and more accurate when I was trying to focus on one child as she played alone or with a group in the classroom. Children shifted their play patterns and areas often, so I had to be prepared to move quickly if I hoped to record an entire sequence of play.

The dual role of teacher and researcher in the classroom had both advantages and disadvantages. Some I had anticipated by reading descriptions of participant-observer methodologies in research books (Schwartzman, 1978; Wright, 1960, 1967). For example, my knowledge of the children and the contexts and antecedents of their play added a depth to my observations that a casual observer would lack. On the other hand, my knowledge of the children and their personalities and backgrounds also carried the potential danger that I might bias what I recorded to remain consistent with my opinion. I felt challenged to raise my awareness of the subjective and objective aspects of my role as a teacher.

Several times the role of recorder interfered with that of classroom teacher. At times, when recording play episodes, I needed to intervene to prevent someone getting hurt or to facilitate a social negotiation among children. Assigning an extra parent-teacher in the classroom to take my role as "floater" resolved this conflict and freed me to finish observations I had begun. For this reason, I believe that both parent cooperatives and teacher-education settings enhance the freedom of teachers to act as researchers because they can rely on other adults as facilitators.

One day, as I was writing an observation of a child nearby, I sat next to another child as she constructed with paper, staples, and tape at a table. The tape dispenser became tangled. She glanced over and saw me taking notes, picked up the tape, and carried it to another adult across the room to ask for help. In other situations, when I was not engaged with my watch, note pad, and pencil, children continued to solicit help or comments from me. When children asked me what I was writing, I'd tell them I was writing down what they did because I was interested in how children played. Sometimes I read them my notes. Thus my data collection in the role of researcher also became an occasion for me to demonstrate the role of reading and writing to children as their teacher.

Although the initial study included only 12 children, it yielded 36 5-minute observations to analyze. In order to reduce the subjective bias about the classroom and the children that I brought to this task, I enlisted the help of a graduate student who was unfamiliar with both the setting and the children and was not a preschool teacher himself. He coded the observations independently of my coding, and then we discussed the discrepancies in our judgments. In such a way, we refined the definitions for types of play and language until we had reached over 90% agreement for each child's observations. This process increased the "reliability" of the research by bringing a different and less biased perspective to the task.

This experience, and a similar one with the four independent coders who helped me with a subsequent study (discussed later), was very valuable to me. Struggling for consensus about the meaning of such terms as "solitary dramatic play" or "self-guiding private speech" not only clarified my research efforts in specific examples, it also expanded my awareness of what I observed as a teacher.

For example, early in the year I had collected observations of Mark, a sophisticated 4-year-old whose play changed over the weeks of the study. His play, once rich in language and fantasy, had become repetitive and physically destructive, both when alone and with other children. I showed his mother the observations and the changes that I had documented. She explained that she had recently begun a family daycare business in their home and that Mark had begun to watch TV cartoons in the morning, as the children were dropped off by their parents. This change in his before-preschool routine, coupled with his probable feelings about the withdrawal of his mother's attention in the morning, was revealed in his play. We agreed on a plan to eliminate morning TV and give him some time alone with his mother. Mark's play soon returned to its former level of sophistication.

From a research perspective, this initial study revealed some interesting differences in the behavior of children of different ages and sexes. First, the girls engaged in more constructive play and the boys in more group dramatic play. Second, comparison of the three age groups (3-year-olds, 4-year-olds, and 5-year-olds) showed an increase in the amount of both parallel play and collective monologue recorded for the fours, and a decrease for the fives. Frequencies of both these categories "peaked" at age 4 and dropped off again from age 4 to 5. Third, sensorimotor/functional play decreased steadily from a high frequency with the threes to a lower frequency with the fives. Both constructive and dramatic play increased in frequency as the average age of the groups increased.

In considering these findings, I realized that most of the boys' observations took place outdoors or in the block area and most of the girls' observations were drawn from the art or small-games area. I turned again to the research literature on play and found that certain types of play are associated with specific areas of the classroom. For example, functional and dramatic group play are frequently observed with outdoor climbing toys. Boys and girls, particularly at ages 4 and 5, tend to segregate themselves by sex into different areas of the classroom and play yard (Goldman, 1981; Hendrickson, Strain, Tremblay, & Shores, 1981; Johnson & Ershler, 1981; Paley, 1984; Roper & Hinde, 1978). It was not clear whether the differences between girls and boys were real differences or simply by-products of the areas where play was recorded. To avoid such confusion, observations for each child needed to be balanced among the areas of the classroom thought to "pull" for different kinds of play.

Efforts to make sense of these findings by reviewing the research literature helped me to refine my techniques as a researcher. My work also attuned me to the patterns of play that differentiated boys from girls and shy children from outgoing ones. For example, I noticed that shy children were more inclined to play in areas such as the blocks or puzzles, where they could comfortably watch others from the outskirts and join group play only as they chose to. My research highlighted other individual differences. My under-standing of skilled and less skilled climbers or riders or painters or builders was enhanced by considering the effects of the physical environment on their choices of activities. Providing opportunities for solitary exploration and practice with materials such as scooters, watercolor paints, or carpentry tools encouraged children who were uncertain of their skills to try new activities alone before having to cope with the demands of a group. Efforts to maintain effectively an unbiased observer stance as a researcher also enabled me as a teacher to be more sensitive to the individual and group needs in my classroom.

LOOKING AT LANGUAGE AND PLAY:
A LARGER STUDY

Drawing on the lessons learned and categories defined in the initial study, I designed and implemented a larger study in the same setting a year later.

sample

After I had explained the study and what would be required of parents and children, 43 of 60 families enrolled in the preschool at that time volunteered to participate. Drawing slips of paper from a hat, I selected at random 36 of those 43 families until I had three groups of children in each of the three age groups, with 6 girls and 6 boys in each group. This "randomization" process alleviated the bias that might come from my subjective reasons for selecting some of the volunteer families over the others.

Group I ranged in age from 2½ to 3½ years old, with an average age of 3 years, 1 month; Group II ranged in age from 3½ to 4½, with an average age of 4 years, 0 months; Group III ranged in age from 4½ to 5½, with an average of 5 years, 0 months.

collecting and organizing data

For this study, two observations were collected in each of three types of play areas:

1. Blocks, art, sand, puzzles, and Leggos; thought to "pull" for constructive play
2. Outdoor and indoor large-muscle toys such as climbing structures, trikes, swings, and tumbling mats and tires; thought to "pull" for functional, rough-and-tumble and dramatic play
3. Housekeeping or thematic props areas such as hospital, spaceship, and farm animals; believed to foster a large proportion of dramatic play

Because this study involved more children, I secured the help of the teacher of the afternoon session to help me in collecting observations. As researchers, we simultaneously recorded children's play behavior for 5-minute periods during the daily 90-minute unstructured play period, when children were free to choose their own activities. Teacher-directed activities such as snack, circle time, and story time were not included in data collection in order to insure that self-initiated activity (even if it were not all play) would be the focus of the study.

Then we compared our observations to determine the amount of agreement in recording the behavior and language of each child we had "targeted" for observation. Two outside judges rated our percentage of agreement in recording events and utterances. We practiced simultaneous observations of "target" children and compared their content until we reached 95% agreement in the events and language we recorded. Periodically, during the 4 months of data collection, we checked our recording with simultaneous observations to determine that we continued to share a perspective on the children's play and language we observed. This procedure allowed us to focus more precisely when writing observations and enhanced the reliability of our data.

using observations in the classroom

As teachers, we used our observations as the basis for assessing and intervening with children in our program, and as food for thought in planning our curriculum. We identified patterns of using toys and activity areas and checked our intuitions about the group differences and individual patterns of behavior we observed.

For example, after noticing that both the 5-year-old boys and 5-year-old girls were playing "Star Wars" but in different places (the girls in the playhouse and the boys in the blocks), we rearranged the classroom to place the two areas adjacent to one another. The boys and girls began to merge their dramatic play and later formed a common ground for "space play" in the outdoor climbing structure.

In addition to observing differences in girls' and boys' play patterns, we also became sensitive to the multi-age interaction in the classroom. It appeared that older children played differently with younger playmates than with same-age peers, and that younger children imitated both the language and roles that their older playmates modeled.

Research by Dunn (1985) and Dunn and Dale (1984) in England indicates that there are many ways that older children engage attention and model pretend play for their younger siblings. The details of such peer-tutoring in play remain an unopened door for future research by teachers in multi-aged preschool settings.

analyzing the play

When all the observations had been collected, the children's names were removed from them and all the observations were numbered to protect the identities of the children. However, all parents received copies of the observations collected on their child to keep as mementos of that time in the child's life. Three years later, I still encounter parents who remark how special it is to be able to go back and read the short vignettes of their children's play and see how they have grown.

After collecting 216 5-minute observations, we were faced with the task of analyzing both children's play and language in some systematic way. The first task was to divide the events of each 5-minute observation, or "protocol," into units that could be classified as "play" or "nonplay" in nature. Nonplay events such as hanging up a coat upon arrival, eating, drinking, or caring for personal needs outside a play frame of reference were excluded from analysis. Emotional events such as crying after falling off a trike or running to greet a parent arriving to claim a child were noted as marking transitions from play episodes but were not analyzed if they were not part of an observable play episode.

A play episode was defined as the child's sustained involvement with play materials, playmates, or roles and usually had some readily identifiable theme such as "building a bridge," "flight to space," or "pouring and molding." Onlooker behavior, defined by Parten (1932), Barnes (1971), and Smith (1978) as "watching and scanning" was not included as play behavior but was analyzed as a separate category.

After identifying thematic episodes, we coded them as solitary, parallel, or group play, following the descriptions presented in Chapter 2 and consistent with the small study previously conducted.

The second step in the coding process was to "layer" the cognitive categories (sensorimotor, constructive, dramatic, and rule-based) onto the social categories, as Rubin and his colleagues (1978) had done. This created 12 possibilities for each play episode: functional, constructive, dramatic, and rule-based solitary play; functional, constructive, dramatic, and rule-based parallel play; and functional, constructive, dramatic, and rule-based group play.

Because 12 categories seemed unwieldy, and because the original question was related to changes in the nature of solitary play, I opted to code only solitary play with the detailed categories of cognitive complexity. I simply noted the frequency of episodes of parallel and rule-based group play, without further analysis into their degrees of cognitive complexity.

analyzing the language

A similar process was used with children's language in the protocols we recorded. First, language was divided into "utterances," according to meaning expressed. Some utterances were complete sentences. Others were single words or nonsense syllables.

Like the play episodes, utterances were first coded for social categories: speech to the self, collective monologue, and speech socially adapted to others. *Speech to the self* is defined as talking aloud in order to communicate to oneself. Such speech provides stimulation or information to the speaker. *Collective monologue* occurs when the speaker uses a social form of speech; that is, the comments appear to be directed to others. But either there is no response from the listener, and the speaker does not pursue one, or the content of speech is not contingent on the listeners' responses. Without listening to the content, an outside observer might infer that a conversation is taking place. In fact, only the form is social, while the content is private. *Socially adapted speech* is language directed to the listener and adapted to the listener's responses. The listener's responses may be verbal or gestural. Much child speech directed to adults or younger children is of this nature.

Categories of cognitive complexity, first described by Piaget (1969) and later refined by Kohlberg, Yaeger, and Hjertholm (1968) were then "layered" onto social speech categories. These categories, comparable to the "distancing" dimension described in children's play, were echolalia, monologue, role-play speech, and self-guiding speech.

Echolalia is defined as self-stimulating speech, often repetition of sounds or phrases. Singing and nonsense syllables repeated in a pattern are common examples of this category.

> Three-year-old Bruce kneels in the sandbox, piling sand into a mound. He chants softly in a singsong rhythm "Bigga, bigga, bigga, big!"

Monologue occurs when the child accompanies his action with a commentary. What is said is dependent on the immediate physical context and serves to parallel action rather than plan for it.

> Three-year-old Peter pats pieces of playdough with his fist. "I'm pounding this away. This playdough right here."

Role-play speech occurs when the perspective of another person is implicit or verbalized. This includes speech to inanimate objects such as dolls or other toys, and dialogues in which the child changes voices or tones to imitate the role of an object, animal, or person.

> Four-year-old Allan picks up a small toy pig and holds it next to a larger pig. Allan says, in a high-pitched tone, "Oink! Oink! Daddy!" Allan then says, in a deep voice, "What is it, little pig?"

Self-guiding speech includes questions posed to the self ("Can I do that?"), comments that guide actions ("I'll try this one now"), and comments that indicate planning ("I'm gonna get some coffee now"). This planning function is what primarily differentiates self-guiding speech from monologue (Wertsch, 1979).

Again, since the focus was on the role of solitary play and private speech, the detailed categories of cognitive complexity were applied only to the observations of speech to the self. Collective monologue an socially adapted speech were recorded without further analysis into levels of cognitive complexity.

reliability of coding

Just as we had needed to determine that we were consistent in our recording of observations, consistency of agreement about the categories for coding was necessary. Although strict statistical reliability is difficult to achieve in participant-observer research, efforts to include the perspectives of others who were outside the setting and not involved in the process of data collection seemed an important check on our perceptions.

Four coders, unfamiliar with the children or with the setting, each coded a portion of the protocols that had been coded by myself and my co-teacher-researcher. Each protocol was coded by two or three people, with disagreements resolved by yet another coder. Fortunately, the pilot study had enabled me to anticipate and clarify many of the overlapping categories of play and language where questions were raised, so that coding was 87% to 96% reliable.

When all the protocols had been coded and the frequencies of each category noted, I calculated the percentage of each child's total responses represented by that category. This enabled me to compare children who played fewer episodes with those who played many. For example, Mark, a 3-year-old, engaged in 17 episodes of play, including 6 of solitary play. Randy, age 4½, also engaged in 6 episodes of solitary play. But for Randy, whose total number of play episodes was fewer, the percentage of solitary play was 6 out of 10, or 60%. For Mark, the same number of play episodes constituted only 35% of the total. Percentages for categories of language were calculated in a similar manner, enabling me to compare children who spoke frequently with those who spoke fewer times.

After calculating percentages for each group of children, I checked to see if the sex differences I had found in the initial study still remained after the precautions had been taken to balance the number of observations according to areas of the classroom and outdoor setting. No significant differences between boys and girls were found for either play or language, so the groups were combined in order to look at the age differences in the study.

findings regarding play

After nearly 6 months of coding and another 6 months of statistical analysis, I returned to the questions that originated in the earliest classroom observations: How did the patterns of children's play and language differ when 3-year-olds were compared to 4- and 5-year-olds? Were solitary play and collective monologue occurring together? How were socially adapted speech and group play related? Finally, how could I use what I found to understand the development of the children I taught?

SOCIAL PLAY. First of all, the "levels" of social play (solitary, parallel, and group) and of language (speech to the self, collective monologue, and speech adapted to others) did not form a hierarchy increasing with age. Thus my findings were similar to previous research on play (Rubin et al., 1978) that used Parten's (1932) categories. These "levels" were more descriptive of *styles* of play that children experienced than degrees of social maturity. Solitary play did not appear to be gradually *replaced* by group play during the preschool years; rather, the shift was in the *relative predominance* of social modes of play as children developed. Among children ages 3 and 4, solitary play was the predominant mode, shifting to group play as the predominant mode for the 5-year-olds, although solitary play remained a common form of play for fours and fives.

As the amount of solitary play declined, the amount of group play steadily increased. Three-year-olds engaged in relatively little parallel or group play; for them, solitary and onlooker behavior predominated. Four-year-olds played nearly as often in solitary, group, and parallel play modes. Five-year-olds played alone or with a group most often and seldom played parallel to one another.

These trends lend support to the idea that solitary play for 3-year-olds may reflect limitations on their ability to interact with others. Rather than disappearing as a mode of play, solitary play for the 5-year-old becomes a choice. Most 5-year-olds shift easily between group and private play.

One implication for teachers is that 3-year-olds may need to play alone until they are ready to begin imagining the perspectives of others and can truly understand the idea of "sharing." Another implication lends guidance to the teacher of 5-year-olds. A 5-year-old who is unable to shift from solitary to group play or who engages in much parallel play may be reflecting social skills more characteristic of a younger child. The teacher might intervene to help her enter group play and coordinate the perspectives of others with her own. The teacher would also remain sensitive to the child's need to enter the more comfortable and familiar mode of solitary play or to use parallel play as a transition to playing with others.

PARALLEL PLAY. One of the most interesting patterns in this research was the change in the frequency of parallel play. Parallel play increased when 4-year-olds were compared with threes, then decreased sharply when fours were compared with fives. Barnes (1971), Mueller & Brenner (1977), and Parten (1932) found similar trends in their research. Parallel play thus may represent a category of social experience that enables children to explore the differences between private and social modes of functioning. Parallel play has been characterized as "private play in a social form" in which children combine the personal proximity and shared materials of group play with the content of a solitary play experience.

Increasing experience with peers in these ambiguously defined parallel situations allows children to differentiate the requirements of group play from those of solitary play and to integrate the perspectives of peers as they consolidate actions and themes at their own pace. Many children will engage in solitary play with a new material or theme until activities with the object or theme have become consolidated in their behavior. With the secure base of a familiar material or theme, a child may then choose to focus her energy on integrating the perspectives of others as well. Alternatively, the presence of a secure and familiar playmate (perhaps a sibling) in parallel play may provide the base for exploring a new play scheme without the demands of social interaction. Both social interaction and play schemes require mental effort and distancing to be successful. The young child may need to practice such effort in sequence rather than all at once. So, in the case of Ronnie described at the beginning of this chapter, the social requirements of sharing and playing with the blocks simultaneously was too much to ask.

Another implication is that parallel play may vary with the age of the child's playmate. With same-age playmates, children may not easily discriminate subtle borders between self and other. They make assumptions about their peers in a shared context of meaning that is not clearly defined. With playmates who are obviously younger or older, children may see the more obvious differences in shared meanings and show sensitivity to the perspectives of others.

> Two-year-old Mike is playing with his 5-year-old sister Kathy and a 4-year-old playmate Sam. Sam walks into the room and addresses Mike, who is standing aside from the ongoing play in the room, watching. "Hey Mikie, Mikie, Boy!" Sam turns to Kathy, who is playing "Star Wars" with two other children, "Let's let Mike be R2D2!" Kathy responds, "O.K. I can pick him up. Hey, Mikie, can big sister pick you up?" She struggles to lift Mike, but is unsuccessful. She says, "Well, just come on in the hideout with us. You have to be a boy robot."

In addition to providing opportunities for children to explore private and social forms of play, parallel play also serves as a nonthreatening entry into group play for many children.

> Karen (4 years, 2 months) approaches Brad who is sitting on top of the stairs. He has opened a lunch box that is filled with paper. Karen picks up a piece of paper and holds it to her mouth, smacking her lips. "Yum, yum," she says, smiling shyly at Brad.

Some children enter play "through the back door," as Karen did, while others use parallel play as a means of enticing less sophisticated players into a dramatic play sequence.

> David (5 years, 2 months) is in the playhouse with Kris (3 years, 2 months). He goes out and picks up a large toy snake, and says, "Pet snake! Pet snake! Pet snake! Hey honey!" He brings the snake into the house. Kris continues to put together a puzzle, kneeling on the floor. David reaches in the oven. "O.K.! Those cupcakes are finished" He closes the oven and glances toward Kris.

ONLOOKER BEHAVIOR. Like Mike, many of the younger children in the study watched at the "edges" of play in the classroom, without attempting to join in. The frequency of such behavior declined as the average age of the children studied increased. Rubin (1982) notes that teachers generally consider this onlooker behavior "benign" rather than indicative of social incompetence. However, he found that children who watch rather than participate are less mature chronologically and mentally than those who choose to participate.

In my study, two distinct patterns of onlooker behavior emerged. The first was typical of younger children who seemed to "watch and scan" (Smith, 1978), in order to gather information about behaviors appropriate to social contexts.

> Mary (2 years, 11 months) picks up a bean bag from the shelf, sets it on the steps, then crawls under the steps, watching Robin construct a house of cardboard bricks.

> Kristine (3 years, 4 months) walks slowly into the tumbling room, hands in her pockets. Alice invites her to play store with them. Kristine approaches the table with the cash register and stands with her hands in her pockets, watching.

On the other hand, older children engaged in such on-looker behavior less frequently and with the apparent purpose of selecting among alternative social choices, or perhaps of finding an appropriate entry into the ongoing play sequence they observed.

> Alice (4 years, 8 months) dries her hands on a paper towel, throws it away, and strolls into the activity room. She pauses to watch several children playing a board game, then watches a group in the playhouse. She enters the playhouse, laughing, and taps Kevin on the head: "Knock-knock."

Teachers who observe such behavior in young children may want to facilitate the child's "information-gathering" or "choice-making" process by talking to her about what is perceived, guiding her to imagine ways that she could participate.

findings regarding language

Turning to the analysis of children's language, I was surprised to find that the frequency of speech to the self did not differ significantly in comparing the three age groups, indicating that such speech may be common to many ages. What *does* apparently change is the ability to determine in what social situations private and social forms of speech are expected. Preschool children are just developing the sense of how social context and speech patterns go together, and many talk to themselves in situations that adults or older children would find embarrassing.

The frequency of children's speech adapted to others also did not change with age. Careful study of the protocols, however, showed that there *were* differences in the ways that older and younger children use socially adapted language. For example, 3-year-olds typically used language adapted to others to discuss or negotiate taking turns with concrete objects.

> Two 3-year-olds are engaged in parallel play with dollhouse materials. Hillary says, "What's this, Jason?" Jason replies, "It's stairs. You walk up it."

The 4- and 5-year-old children used socially adapted speech in more cognitively abstract ways, discussing and negotiating shared play themes and roles.

> Amy and Ruth are playing "Star Wars" on the climbing structure. Amy has taken the role of Princess Leia. Ruth wants to take the same role. Amy suggests that Ruth could be "Princess Leia's sister," and Ruth agrees. Ruth goes to the shelf and selects a large straw hat with ribbons that tie. She asks a participating parent, "Will you tie this on for me?" The adult ties the hat, and Ruth returns to the "spaceship." Amy turns and comments, "Princess Leia doesn't have a hat." "I *know*," responds Ruth. "And neither does her sister!" retorts Amy. Ruth reluctantly takes off the hat and returns it to the shelf. She picks up an apron and holds it to her waist, commenting, "Princess Leia's sister needs this to cook!"

Older children also spoke to one another consistent with the roles they played and in harmony with the role identities and language spoken by the other players.

> Alice (4 years, 6 months), Ann (3 years, 6 months) and Marty (4 years, 5 months) are playing "Star Wars." Alice exclaims, "They hurt me, Luke!" Marty asks, "Who did?" Alice answers, "The storm troopers! Help! Help! My hands are tied up." To Ann, she says, "Oh, Space Kitty, we're stuck! Get your claws and get the rope off us!"

Teachers of young children may facilitate more abstract representation in social speech by encouraging children to verbalize their thoughts to others. Younger preschoolers will most often share ideas about concrete objects in their play. Older preschoolers can be encouraged to verbalize thoughts about shared experiences (both real and pretend) and roles and themes implicit in their dramatic play. Teachers can also help children to use language consistent with the roles they play and to make that language contingent upon the complementary roles of others.

I am reminded of the 4-year-old who was hooked on the "Dukes of Hazzard" television show. He consistently approached playmates with the line, "C'mon Beau. Let's go!" and ran off, expecting his peer to follow. Teachers can encourage children whose play dialogue is limited to repetitive one-liners to extend their imagination and language contingent on responses to others. In this way they may mitigate the effects of stereotyped television characterizations and encourage the interplay of abstract ideas typical of the older preschooler.

Another interesting finding was that, as with parallel play, the amount of collective monologue increased with 4-year-olds as compared to threes, and decreased with fives compared to fours. Collective monologue and parallel play may be viewed as adaptive behavior for children learning to interact with their peers. They contribute to children's growing discrimination between private and social forms of communication and contexts appropriate to each form. Collective monologue reflects speech intended to communicate meaning to oneself, but in the form of speaking aloud to others, just as parallel play reflects private play in a social form. As private and social play and speech become more differentiated, children plan what they are going to do or say and make predictions about the responses they may expect from others. For example, "You're my friend, right?" or, "I'll be the mom, okay?" are both utterances that call for a response.

Preschool teachers often characterize age 4 as the "golden age of fantasy." This is the age when play with the peer group begins to take precedence over solitary play, and yet private and social forms of symbolic expression are mixed. As the 4-year-old experiences this mixture of forms in contexts of shared meaning, both parallel play and collective monologue increase in frequency.

At 5, children not only mentally represent the perspectives of other people but coordinate those representations with their own viewpoints. This increase in the ability to think abstractly enables the 5-year-old to engage in complicated multidimensional play episodes with others and to discriminate situations in which private and social forms of expression are most appropriate.

findings regarding levels of cognitive complexity in play and language

Examination of the number of episodes classified according to the cognitive complexity of the solitary play (functional, constructive, dramatic, and rule-based), indicated that complexity increased with age. The same pattern was true for the cognitive complexity dimensions applied to self-speech (echolalia, monologue, role-play speech, and self-guiding speech).

In both their solitary play and their self-speech, older children functioned at higher levels of cognitive complexity. Rubin and colleagues (1978) reported similar findings with regard to children's play, suggesting that a large proportion of functional solitary play is typical of young preschoolers. With age, preschoolers integrate increasingly abstract elements into their play and sustain themes for long periods of time through the use of language.

Another finding was that, as the number of play episodes decreased among the older children, the number of utterances increased. As children become able to use more complex language in their play, their episodes become longer, more complex, and less dependent on the use of concrete objects. Language enables them to extend the realms of their imaginations.

RULE-BASED PLAY. As expected, solitary play at games with rules was not a common category in this study (only one instance was observed). Such episodes of group play were fairly common in the observations of older preschoolers. Piaget (1965) reported that the first games with rules appeared in group play at age 5.

From Mead's (1934) point of view, games with rules are learned in a social context. Only with extensive experience at coordinating rules of a game with the perspective of oneself and the other players do children "code" these experiences completely enough to play them out in a solitary context.

As a prelude to rule-based play, solitary dramatic play requires a child to represent both his own perspective and that of another person within a solitary context. Some children use dolls, toys, or imaginary friends to "anchor" their representations of the viewpoints of others. Solitary games with rules require a child to represent and coordinate perspectives of himself and other players and to apply the framework of the rules. Representation and coordination of all these elements simultaneously is beyond the intellectual capacity of most preschool children. However, older preschoolers will occasionally play a board game or card game alone (or with a toy), showing the beginning of their understanding of the complex thinking involved in games with rules.

The implications of this finding are that games with formal rules, such as lotto, Candyland, and other commercial board games may not be developmentally appropriate for preschool children, if they are presented in a rigidly structured manner. If children are encouraged to construct their own games with rules, using materials in a manner similar to dramatic play, both the educational content and the rules of the game will be more meaningful to children, as they develop concepts and negotiate strategies. As a teacher, I found this idea of asking children to create their own rules for commercial or teacher-made games enhanced their thinking and my sensitivity to their needs.

My favorite example is 4½-year-old Sally, who played alone with the board game Candyland for nearly 30 minutes. She carefully set out all the cards, on the floor, face-up, in neat rows. She then opened the board and placed the plastic markers at the start. I watched her scan the rows of cards and pick up her marker. At that moment, she noticed me observing and invited me to play. She explained, "First you have to pick a bunny or something to be your marker thing. Then you look at the board, see where you want to go, and pick the card that matches it!" Sally had reversed the order of the matching process in the commercial rules for the game and used the board as a "map" for the players' desires rather than as a route to winning the game. "Winning" for Sally meant that the players continued to move to their favorite places on the board until all the cards were taken, or they became tired of the game. This concept was readily embraced by the others who were drawn into the game as I had been.

SELF-GUIDING SPEECH. In terms of cognitive categories applied to speech, only self-guiding speech increased significantly with age. Self-guiding speech incorporates two important aspects of development; that is, it requires a level of mental representation that enables the child to encode the meaning of an utterance and simultaneously to predict a response from another person, an object, or a sequence of events.

> Five-year-old Jake says, in a low voice to himself, "O.K. Now I'll find that cape. Then I'll be a Superhero too!"

Presumably, the self-guiding speech of older preschoolers, spoken aloud, reflects the overt form of dialogue that will later become silent inner speech. For younger children, monologue seems to have much the same function as self-guiding speech without the element of planfulness or predicting future events.

> Jill (3 years, 4 months) washes her doll's arms and legs with a baby wipe. She stands the doll up facing her, saying, "I'm trying to dress my baby."

It may be that the planning nature of self-guiding speech is layered onto the essentially self-guiding nature of monologue as children's capacity for mental abstraction grows. Monologue speech was common across the three age groups studied, while self-guiding speech increased after age 4.

ROLE-PLAY SPEECH. When children's role-play speech to themselves was analyzed, two types emerged. The first involved questions asked and answered by the child in a task-related situation.

> Miles, age 4½, is sitting alone on the rug in the classroom, putting together a wooden puzzle. He speaks to himself in a low voice: "Now, where does this piece go? It's in the left part of the right." He places a piece in the puzzle frame. It fits. "Ah ha! Here, I got you!"

The second kind of role-play speech emerged in solitary dramatic play episodes and involved communications with imaginary others.

> Marty (4 years, 6 months) is playing alone in the sandbox. In a soft voice, he says, "Well, I'm Lord of the Jungle. That's why I'm Tarzan!" He jumps up, crouches, then looks over his left shoulder. "C'mon Cheetah! Let's run!"

Each type of role-play speech involved coordinating perspectives of the self-as-the-speaker with the self-as-the-listener in a situation, but the first showed a directive role in problem solving, while the second used an open-ended role in fantasy play.

As with self-guiding speech, the overt enactment of roles of self and others in hypothetical situations is thought to be less common in middle childhood, when children carry out personal fantasy in their minds. From personal observation and conversations with parents, this developmental difference may only be true for some social contexts. Older children perceive that overt expression of fantasy is inappropriate in some group contexts (for example, when eating at the lunch table), yet they may engage in overt role-play speech when alone, with siblings, or with close friends.

Perhaps speech does not become totally interiorized or socialized, even for adults. Many adults report talking to themselves when alone. Forms of collective monologue, such as asking a question without expecting a response, are common among adults who have intimate shared contexts of meaning.

The findings for the cognitive complexity of self-speech have implications for teachers' use of questioning strategies with young children. Implicit dialogue between the self and an imagined "other" helps children coordinate perspectives of the self-as-speaker and the self-as-listener, and to predict responses. Teachers who are skilled in framing questions rather than directives may facilitate children's transition from reliance on others to reliance on guidance from themselves.

In addition, teachers who participate in role-play dialogues with young children, assuming roles that complement children's make-believe roles, provide experiences that will lead children to coordinate the perspectives of others with their own. They support children's efforts to converse in social situations and to create imaginary narratives in literature and play.

REFLECTING ON THE RESEARCH PROCESS

I began with efforts to understand children's needs to play alone, to *not* share sometimes, and to converse aloud with themselves or an imagined playmate. I thought that, by carefully observing the children in my classroom and reading what researchers and theorists had to say, my questions might be answered. But the answers were incomplete and unsatisfactory. The more information I discovered, the more paradoxical behaviors such as solitary play and private speech appeared. Even reading the research literature that seemed comprehensive and intuitively valid to me as a teacher did not draw implications for practice in my classroom.

These factors, combined with my fascination of diverse theoretical positions on the development of play and language, enticed me into the role of researcher. I slowly familiarized myself with the tools and techniques of formal research. I struggled with such concepts as reliability, coding, and statistical significance. I carefully considered ethical ideas such as confidentiality and informed consent. The challenge of collecting data without intruding upon children or short-changing my responsibilities as their teacher took months to resolve.

Analyzing the data, although time-consuming, was rewarding and often pleasurable. My understanding of the complexity of thought and interaction in the play of young children grew daily and was complemented by the amusement I felt in rereading reports of their activities. Now that I no longer teach in a preschool classroom, I savor the vignettes of the children's behavior as I draw upon them as examples to help new teachers understand play and language development.

The most valuable lesson was that research need not be a mystical, cerebral process removed from the lives of real children and teachers. As a teacher conducting my own research, I realized how important my specific questions regarding the development of children were. Research I had read early on simply did not ask the same questions I asked. My analysis, too, was qualitatively different. Although I applied formal statistical analyses, the real joy came in thinking about how the findings from my study would guide teachers to support more fully the development of language and play in their own settings.

This chapter describes only two studies. Their contribution to the research literature in early childhood education is modest. But the example my process provides for other teachers who ask questions about children in their own classrooms may encourage them to embark on a similarly rewarding and challenging experience.

5
play: the child's unseen curriculum

BY BARBARA SCALES

I once heard the term "angel's hair" used to describe the researcher's dilemma in studying play. Visually palpable, play, like angel's hair, is so ephemeral that it seems to vanish when examined. At my school, my colleagues and I found that play, studied systematically as it naturally occurs, does not vanish; instead, a valuable and unseen curriculum for socialization appears.

Some puzzling aspects of play and our planning for it that intrigued us and served as impetus for study are illustrated in the following anecdotes:

An attractive deck, built around a large shade tree in our play yard, failed to appeal to children. Later, when teachers stooped to take a child's eye view, they found that the deck and its access points virtually disappeared. This leafy retreat, designed for quiet pretend play, had meaning for an adult but was as visually "out of context" for children as the top of the refrigerator in my own home was for me.

A group of children gathered around their teacher at the juice table were interrupted by three children, attired in fire hats and brandishing hoses, who boisterously entered the room intent on quenching a fire. The teacher tried to reorient them with the indirect commentary, "You must have forgotten your inside voices."

In an attempt to clarify roles in a dramatic play event involving a larger-than-usual number of children, the teacher asked, "Who are the robbers and who are the police?" One child answered, "I'm a robber *and* a policeman."

In the second example, what led the teacher to assume that children would comprehend her indirect reference to the context-appropriateness of their play? In the third example, how should she respond to what appears to be a confusion of roles?

Three $4\frac{1}{2}$-year-old boys have created a game of "stealing crackers" from the juice room. With exaggerated whispers and stealthy glances they transport their "loot" to a hideout in an area of the play yard reserved for active play. The crackers are seldom actually eaten, although repeated forays for replenishment gleefully occur.

We wondered what was going on during this play and whether we should enter into it.

This chapter describes the ways that my research on play revealed how both the physical and the social features of the school environment intersect to influence children's play behavior. It shows how children communicate their knowledge and understanding of appropriateness rules (the implied expectations of the school setting) to their peers in play. It demonstrates how children's sharing of such implied expectations supports their play interactions. As apprentices to a social world, children, lacking fully developed linguistic and communicative abilities, are initially unable to establish and maintain play themes. Sharing gradually imparts cohesiveness to the themes they bring to their play.

Nursery-school teachers have traditionally assumed that self-directed play is a major vehicle for socialization. Within the last 10 years, research on play has begun to uncover some of the actual mechanisms involved in this socialization, revealing how configurations of social and environmental features interact to shape and support, or restrict and constrain, children's spontaneous play communication. Most recently, researchers, some in collaboration with teachers, have begun using methods that can be adapted to entering the child's world to observe play interactions in natural contexts (Corsaro, 1985; Florio & Walsh, 1981; Genishi, 1983). Other researchers have replicated specific features of play under laboratory (or standardized) conditions to investigate children's communicative competence and social understanding (Damon, 1977; Denzin, 1977; Garvey, 1977; Nucci & Turiel, 1978).

Nursery-school teachers have always assumed that children playing at pretense in the housekeeping corner or quietly engrossed with a companion in the block corner or moving swiftly with playmates on a climbing structure are engaged in serious business. Research now shows that children's interactions provide an opportunity for teachers to observe the process by which the child's social self emerges. In independent or collaborative research, teachers find the ways to verify their intuitions about play and researchers find evidence to ground empirically theories about the function of play. A number of recent studies showing how language and social knowledge intersect have involved such collaboration (Florio & Walsh, 1981; Gilmore & Glatthorn, 1982).

Current studies of children's language and communication are paralleled by earlier research with adults. Theoretical work by Cicourel (1974), Goffman (1974), Gumperz (1982a, 1982b), and others reveals the complex processes at work in normal everyday interactions such as adult conversations. The strategies we use for conducting conversations with others are a little like the air we breathe: invisible. We only notice them in their absence, that is, when there is a breach in the normal course of our experience. Factors that influence play and socialization in the nursery school are also invisible in much the same way and constitute an "unseen curriculum."

THE NEED FOR MAKING THE UNSEEN CURRICULUM VISIBLE

Research on "hidden curricula" shows that children coming from different ethnic or class groups are socialized and educated differently, despite egalitarian aims (Archer & Lloyd, 1985). Interestingly, such differential treatment and children's responses to it seem to lie outside of the teacher's conscious intent or awareness.

Processes of socialization start very early in infancy and are embedded in the ways humans communicate and conduct their everyday affairs. We learn to modify the way we address a baby or respond to his cooings and gurgles. We acquire formulas for addressing unseen partners in telephone conversations. A contemporary example is wondering whether we should omit "thank you" when we are addressed by a computer "voice" on the telephone.

In normal discourse we mark the status of others and find ways of indicating a shared history such as family, ethnic, or cultural group identity. We know there are variations in ways that membership in a common or particular group are to be marked in interaction. We have repertoires or routines for introducing, maintaining, or altering themes in everyday discourse. These important elements of human communication and interaction seem to be unconsciously acquired and have recently become of interest to researchers.

The study of speech alone — its grammar, accent, inflection, text, or content — will not reveal the rules for interaction; nor will examination of nonverbal elements or "body language" alone reveal the processes at work. Critical aspects of communication involve an array of co-occurring elements that appear for the most part to be self-taught. They vary across cultural and ethnic groups as well as gender and age; some are evident in very early communicative repertoires of children (Ericksen, 1977; Gumperz, 1982b). For example, Ryan (1974) and others have found that the rhythmic patterns of inflection in the babbling of babies vary culturally and correspond to the inflection of the parents' speech.

Instruction in communicative skills that encompass these features is not overt and exists at home and in schools as unseen curriculum. The difference in the socialization of boys and girls is just beginning to be understood. Lack of knowledge in this area raises complex issues for the educator who wishes to be egalitarian with respect to gender. For example, the ways that girls interact with the teacher and relate to teacher-directed activities in the classroom may appear to complement educational goals, but in fact may hamper the growth of independent initiative. On the other hand, teachers' reactions to boys' seemingly more aggressive patterns of interaction may interfere with an understanding of how boys establish their social identity with respect to gender. American classrooms, with their emphasis on individual achievement and self-expression, may run counter to the cultural heritage of some students, where cultural membership and group identity take precedence over individual identity. Often, unconscious assumptions with respect to class or status are made on the basis of inflection, speech style, accent, or dialect. Failure to make this aspect of the curriculum visible often allows invidious role definitions with respect to gender, class, race, or competence to be employed by adults and appropriated by children unconsciously. Despite good intentions, specific educational remedies for inequalities that hamper socialization cannot be effective without knowledge of the diverse mechanisms that operate in communication.

THE PLAY YARD AS A SETTING FOR STUDIES OF PLAY

What follows is an account of the discovery of an unseen curriculum for play at the school at which I work. The research involved only one classroom of 26 children at a university-based child study center, but it suggests how teachers, using available resources, can begin to answer their own questions about play.

The program for 3- and 4-year-olds at my school is planned and implemented by two head teachers, myself, and a colleague, who screen and interview graduate students for positions as assistants. Once employed, assistants participate in a preliminary orientation as well as ongoing staff development and training. They spend 4 hours a day at the center, including 2½ hours in the classroom, with the balance of the time spent in set-up and/or restoration of the classroom and participation in daily evaluations and weekly planning sessions. The staff of graduate-student assistants work as a team. Curriculum is often generated by their competencies and interests, the needs of the children, and staff discussion. The school is relatively balanced ethnically; however, parents are primarily professionals from upper- or middle-class backgrounds, with a few blue-collar occupations represented.

I, like most nursery-school educators, believe that the nursery school provides a curriculum for the development of the "whole child"; that learning proceeds in an integrated way and involves all dimensions — social, affective, intellectual, and physical. I and my colleagues believe that the nursery-school classroom is a place where children can learn in a wholesome and natural way through opportunities for guided and self-directed play. Our play yard is seen as an extension of this concept.

The need to restore and replace deteriorating play yard struc-tures provided an opportunity to study how effectively the play yard supported the school's goals for learning and social develop-ment in play. We wanted to improve the quality of play and learn more about how the existing equipment supported or constrained it.

In preparation for talks with designers and play equipment specialists, we set out to prepare a rationale for the existing play yard curriculum, identifying those areas where desired forms of play occurred. Surprisingly, this process involved more time and thought than we anticipated. We found, in articulating our rationale, that practice was based largely upon what had "always been done." There were a number of things for children to do at various locations; quite a lot of things, in fact. These "things to do" were adapted from time-honored traditions: arts and crafts; gardening and pets; domestic or house play; constructive and imaginative play with blocks, small toys, trucks, and shovels; ample and safe opportunities to run, jump, and climb.

In general, the play yard differed from the classroom in emphasis upon large motor activity, noise level, freedom of movement, and the amount of "messy" materials such as sand and water that were permitted. Our underlying assumption was that, if the right elements were present, the desired learning or developmental outcomes would occur. In the process of examining our play yard and attempting to write a curriculum, other, more specific, questions about what we were doing arose.

Why, for example, was a rocking boat that generated loud squeals and vigorous activity placed near a quiet home play area? How was this equipment (generally perceived by children to be a rocket ship) related to our play expectations for the adjoining area? Why were blocks that were always neatly stacked on a platform under partial shelter either ignored by children or appropriated by one group or another to be used as an exclusive territory? Why did play in a large sandpit, the largest and most central element of the yard, seem unfocused, despite frequent intervention?

As we pondered these questions, we also became intrigued with differences between the 3- and 4-year-olds' play. What caused the fours, unlike the threes, to neglect well-equipped domestic play areas such as a small sand table, preferring instead to create their own "houses," "camps," and "hideouts" from toys and bits gathered from all corners of the school? How were we to explain 4-year-old "uprisings," manifesting themselves in group refusal to participate willingly in previously well-established "rituals" such as clean-up and story and group time? How could teachers anticipate and respond to such variations in play patterns as children matured?

The literature on play environments and play yards provided partial answers to these questions. Research conducted at Pacific Oaks College (Kritchevsky & Prescott, with Walling, 1969) had defined play elements on a continuum from simple to complex and devised methods for computing numbers of play spaces available in the environment. Harms and Clifford (1980) had designed an environmental rating scale that could be used to graph the nursery-school environment on the basis of the presence or absence of desired elements. Cognitive development and stage theories of play derived or adapted from Parten (1932), Smilansky (1968), or Piaget (1962), could be invoked to account for differences between the play of younger and older children.

These partial answers generated a lively interest in the play yard among our staff of student assistants. They conducted small studies and surveys, observed children's play, discussed alternatives, and made adjustments and refinements in the play yard. We attempted to maximize and balance the diversity of opportunities for self-directed play across the yard, so children would experience a variety of forms of play.

THE PLAY YARD STUDY GROUP

Following several months of modification of the environment, we began to think of how we could measure more systematically the variations in play patterns that were the result of our modifications. Where were the most self-directed play events occurring? Was the duration of play longer at a small sand table with realistic props or at a large climber where play seemed more fluid and open? If we had a way of contrasting numbers of children playing and the duration of peer interactions in play that occurred at various points in the yard, we thought we could pinpoint areas where the curriculum generated the more successful social interactions. We could make changes and then assess once again.

To help with this task we were joined by a small group of university faculty advisors from the university's anthropology, landscape architecture, and sociology departments. We began to meet and talk regularly and soon began calling ourselves the "Play Yard Study Group."

Previous research at our nursery school had defined various areas in the classroom as "play ecologies" (Cook-Gumperz & Corsaro, 1976). Underlying the idea of a play ecology was the notion that the environment itself offered an "implicit curriculum." Its features suggested things to do through appropriate materials that were near at hand. For example, low shelves with miniature toys arranged on them and placed adjacent to a low table represented a set of environmental cues that were expected to suggest specific kinds of play and indirectly discourage other kinds. This idea complemented an already established practice in nursery-school education traditionally expressed in provisions for a "reading corner," a "block corner," or a "housekeeping corner," and more recently framed in the terms "open classroom," the "learning center," or the "responsive environment." These reflect developmentalists' beliefs that children learn best in active engagement or interaction with the environment and that the child's interest and involvement are the best guide to the kinds of activities that are suited to the individual learner.

the environment as curriculum
for social interaction

We drew on this idea by refining the implicit curriculum found in the environmental features of the play yard to enhance the opportunities for social development we believed occurred in sociodramatic play. By presenting a sufficiently balanced variety and number of options for play, we tried to avoid overcrowding or neglect of play areas. We tried to provide, with a minimum of intervention, opportunities for an optimal amount of self-directed and focused peer interaction. Through the self-organization of their own play occasions, children could develop an understanding of the social regulation of interpersonal relations.

In preparing options for play we considered the need for sufficient staff, area-by-area supervision, and a balance of environmental features. We wanted to provide play situations and unobtrusive adult support for solitary and parallel play as well as group activities, and for varying and changing activities as well as opportunity for maintenance of a single activity across time.

From such an environment we expected the following developmental outcomes:

Self-achievement and mastery
Learning through adult imitation
Affective development through fantasy
Sociolinguistic and verbal development through interaction

Through exchanges among the members of the Play Yard Study Group, a notion of a network of a series of "ecologies" began to emerge. The small sand table, the large sandpit, and the large climber were identified as the three major ecologies. Naturally, teachers began to think in terms of these as they worked in the school. Objectives for each of these three major ecologies began to evolve in staff and study group meetings. We scrutinized existing play materials and equipment for their relevance to expectations for play in each ecology.

assessing play yard activity

Discussion by the Play Yard Study Group continued to focus on ways of assessing what went on in the play yard. We noticed that, although the nursery-school curriculum for play was essentially implied rather than specific, children in large part appeared to understand our expectations for play at each setting. In the classroom, the housekeeping corner generally saw housekeeping play, the work tables generally saw constructive work with various craft materials, and so on. Outdoors, some exceptions were seen in the large sandpit, for instance, where teachers' cues for play failed to attract and hold children's interest in expected ways. Props such as shovels and trucks did not generate the kind of constructive play teachers anticipated. Fast-paced superhero play and attempts to use sand for housekeeping play showed a lack of thematic focus.

We reasoned that the communicative behaviors of the children could provide us with access to their world. Observation and analysis of children's interactive behaviors offered the means for assessing the effectiveness of the nursery school's "implied curriculum" for play. They also provided information needed for making changes that would relate to children's self-generated play themes.

INITIATING A PILOT STUDY

A small pilot study applied this approach. We used 8-mm film to collect records of play that could be studied easily. The camera was focused continuously on the children in the play yard, simultaneously recording the time. The films were then examined and all instances of interactive behavior were recorded by observers.

At any given time a particular child might be interacting only with the physical environment, that is, engaged in solitary play, or she might be interacting with a teacher, or moving from one area of the play yard to another. Most important for the purposes of this study, she might be interacting with another child, as evidenced by such behaviors as leaning toward, speaking to, looking at another child, touching, gazing, holding, or using an object or toy with another child. Such behaviors were cues used to distinguish socially interactive behavior from other behaviors. Since children of these ages express themselves through their bodies as much as through their words, silent film was adequate for this pilot study.

The frequency of socially interactive behaviors was determined by counting the number of children engaged in them at a particular time and place. Summing these numbers gave the frequency for individual children or for a particular ecology. Systematically noting whether or not a child who was engaged in social interaction at one time was still so engaged at the beginning of the next 5-minute interval provided a rough measure of the duration of the social interaction. Duration, and not just frequency, indicates children's social or interactive competence. It reflects children's ability to initiate and maintain discourse over time.

The simple method of logging interactive behaviors at 5-minute intervals gave us a way of assessing the extent to which the children in a given area played together and stayed together. In other words, it enabled us to look at the effectiveness of the areas in supporting the cohesiveness of peer interaction. We were fortunate to have the children's behavior recorded on film, but recording could also have been done by hand, using a stopwatch and pencil and paper.

From this modest study we discovered that some areas of the play yard were less frequented by children or were the site of fewer interactive behaviors. Some areas, such as the swings, accommodated more solitary or onlooker behavior. The pilot study showed which play ecologies should be altered to balance the overall distribution of children playing in the yard. As described earlier, we tried to make neglected areas more attractive or visually salient, defining them as spatial configurations or enclosures. By limiting the available props and accessories to certain themes, we made our expectations for the area clearer. This reduced overcrowding in some areas and the neglect of others and made utilization of staff and school resources more efficient.

Since observations for this study had been collected on silent film, the verbal features of children's interactions were not available for analysis. The thematic content of observed play interactions and the discourse strategies children employed to initiate or maintain their play episodes were not distinguishable. The occurrence and boundaries of sociodramatic play episodes could not be determined. In order for teachers to intervene in the children's play in specifically relevant ways, we needed to be able to analyze the thematic content of play events.

CONDUCTING A SECOND STUDY

A second, more ambitious study was designed that provided a record over a year's time of children's verbal as well as nonverbal play behavior. This second study was oriented to a particular educational philosophy. We believed the communicative strategies children came to use in peer play were shaped by and derived meaning from both the social and physical properties of various situations. The physical properties of settings are obvious, the social less so. Each child brings to a particular situation an understanding of its possibilities that is based on her social experience outside the school as well as inside. The meaning each school situation has is not static but changes and is refined and amplified as the child encounters other children. The communicative behaviors of the children are the medium through which the social world of the nursery school is constructed.

The children of the child study center were again the subjects; however, this time only the 3-year-old class was studied. As in the 4-year-old class, the staff consisted of one head teacher and a team of graduate-student assistants. This class met in the morning, enabling me to have more time to note what was going on, since I was not responsible for teaching at this time.

method of observation

The university media department provided video equipment so that a second, more extensive set of observations of the school play yard could be obtained. Three video cameras located on low rooftops adjacent to the play yard recorded observations of play at the three major play ecologies simultaneously. These records included sound, providing a basis for more systematic and expanded replication of the pilot work. Observational work was conducted in this manner for one hour daily for one week during each of three intervals: the fall, winter, and spring quarters. Video cameras were in full view of children and their parents but did not disrupt the children's normal activities. Parents had been informed about the aims of the study and gave their consent. Questions about the study could be readily answered since we could refer to the videotape record. During taping sessions parents and children often enjoyed viewing the recording on monitors in the school kitchen. Since the study spanned a year's time, most of these 3-year-olds turned 4 before it ended.

setting: the reorganized play yard

As a consequence of the work of the Play Yard Study Group and our pilot study, we now had a clear idea of our curriculum for the play yard as well as its rationale and a set of well-defined objectives. To facilitate self-directed learning, the nursery-school play yard was organized around three major ecological settings. Each setting contained equipment and accessories that reflected a set of expectations founded on teachers' learning objectives for children, their understanding of the developmental needs of children, and what they believed children naturally liked to do in play. One of the major objectives for children in their spontaneous activity was that they would develop greater social competence. This particular aspect of the curriculum was the central subject of the second study. The settings designed to accommodate various forms of social play served as a set of hypotheses about the effect of these environments on the child's socialization.

the three major ecological settings

THE SMALL SAND TABLE. The area of the small sand table, located near the classroom at the northeast side of the playground, had numerous entry points, with heavy traffic flowing on one side from a classroom door adjacent to it. It could accommodate from four to eight children at any one time. The physical objects were sand and water, and the objects with clear social meaning were a small stove, a table, chairs, and dishes and pots.

Teachers generally monitored from a distance. An important expectation for this area was that voices would be moderately quiet; that is, talk was freely tolerated, but yelling loudly was not. The pace of movement was also moderate; for example, dancing was permitted, but running was discouraged. Teachers as well as children relied upon the relevance of communicative behavior to the context or situation to interpret its meaning. By simply participating in a like activity, such as stirring sand or pouring water in a particular way, children often signaled their shared understanding of a play theme. Young children rely equally upon the nonverbal as well as the verbal elements of communication and do not necessarily foreground the linguistic components of communication as adults do. Teachers frequently relied upon the implied expectations of areas to shape the play themes that children generated, rather than directly verbalizing or suggesting appropriate kinds of activities.

Props, equipment, and accessories for this area were those that were known to cue more quiet forms of play. For instance, we had found that work tables or symmetrical play spaces facilitated more quiet and orderly discourse than spaces that were undefined, asymmetrical, or open. The latter spaces required that children have the communicative ability to define and negotiate spatial meaning more fully, to themselves and to each other. In contrast, the small sand table facilitated face-to-face engagement. In this area children generally brought conventional expectations. They derived these from a shared body of knowledge about the meaning of stoves, tables, and miscellaneous kitchen items with respect to roles to be taken and activities to be engaged in. A typical activity perceived as appropriate for this area might be the preparation of food for members of one's family (especially the "children," the "babies," and/or "friends"). A birthday party was a favorite thematic variation. Little verbal communication was needed to sustain the cohesiveness of these play interactions.

THE LARGE SANDPIT. A configuration of tires with four entry points around its outer rim defined the large sandpit, located near the middle of the play yard. Heavy traffic flowed by this area through the center of the play yard and occasionally around its periphery. Large shovels and medium-sized trucks provided opportunity for physical and social contact. The area accommodated four to eight children; however, the usual pattern was two to four. Teachers monitored from a distance and occasionally modeled forms of play or "played" parallel to children here. For example, teachers would pile mounds of sand for tunneling or begin to make channels for water.

Teachers expected play in the large sandpit to be constructive. Digging and shoveling sand as in road making or tunneling were considered appropriate, and the social roles of workers were anticipated in thematic play. Sensorimotor and manipulative play with sand and water also occurred here. The area provided sufficient space for relatively active motor play and supported a moderate to loud level of noise. Aside from play with water and sand, not always possible because of weather conditions, teacher's expectations for focused, cohesive, self-directed play were often unfulfilled in this area.

THE LARGE CLIMBER. The large climber, an enclosed deck mounted on pillars about 7 feet above ground with an A-frame for swings to one side, stood in the far southeast corner of the yard. Entry points included the slide, a wooden ladder, a rope ladder, a fire pole, and a climbing rope. Children occasionally played under or behind this structure. This area also included movable parts such as large boxes, boards, ladders, and blocks, which the teachers arranged in various configurations to adjust for overcrowding on the large climber. The objects were stationary except for accessories children made and brought to the area, such as paper capes, belts, hats, pretend weapons, and occasional fire-play accessories. Cues for specific types of play in this area were relatively neutral. The teacher, usually a supervising teaching assistant also responsible for the large sandpit, monitored from considerable distance most of the time. Active forms of motor play were permitted, and play was often noisy and fast paced. Teachers felt that a major requirement was to be very watchful and alert with respect to safety of the children. Most intervention in children's self-directed play occurred around this issue.

the interactive episode:
a new source of information

In studying the play episodes, we made frequent reference to other researchers who had dealt with communication processes. In doing so, we developed two analytic procedures. First, replicating procedures used in the pilot study, I logged the presence or absence of children engaged in interactive behaviors at 5-minute intervals. I also logged the duration of interactive behavior at the three ecologies. Again, nonverbal cues such as proximity, gaze, body orientation, and exchange of toys distinguished interactive behavior from other behaviors.

The second procedure made use of children's talk to each other, which had become available for analysis in this second study. This source of information made it possible to identify and use interactive episodes as a unit of analysis. In this study an interactive episode is defined as a series of interactive behaviors that have a clearly marked verbal beginning, such as "We're making soup, right?" or "We're friends, right?" After classifying episodes by kind, content, and theme, the frequencies of the various forms of play at the three ecologies were computed, giving us specific information on how children read environmental expectations for play. We could compare and contrast the play yard settings on this dimension and see shifts in forms of thematic play over time. Some episodes showed vividly the kinds of communicative strategies children used to maintain interactive cohesiveness. These episodes demonstrated how social and ecological features influence children's play communication. They also revealed, as communicative competence advanced, how children became able to use language alone to transcend the influence of the ecological features of the setting to create their own social events. For example, as we show later, knowledge of this advance shed light on the "cracker-stealing" incident. We could now account for the transporting of "inside" toys to "outside" camps, hideouts, and homes.

THE MEANING OF "CONTEXT":
A DYNAMIC PROCESS

Our study of the play episodes made clearer to us the features that can be identified in play contexts. We found an adaptation of Keller-Cohen's (1978) categorization of the features of context useful:

1. The situational context
   a. Gestures
   b. Actions
2. The physical context
   a. People
   b. Objects
3. The social context
   a. Setting
   b. Addressee
      i. What the other person is like
      ii. What the other person knows
      iii. What the other person intends
4. The norms of interaction
   a. Knowledge of the rules of interaction that regulate the coordination of the contextual elements
   b. Knowledge of the social rules for speech exchanges in a particular community
      i. Getting another's attention
      ii. Taking turns in talking
      iii. Acknowledging your interlocutor's utterances
      iv. Sustaining the interaction, by being as informative, clear, and relevant as necessary and trying to make contributions that are appropriate and true.

Ervin-Tripp (1983) has said that the play environment provides a scaffolding or framework for children's interactive play. The social and physical properties of settings imply potential play schemes. She argues that

> These activities not only make possible the child's display of language knowledge, but create some conditions for the child to learn to understand new words and new constructions, to imitate, to recall, and try to extend what is known. Learning derives not just from speaking

but from hearing language used in a context where the meaning is obvious and where the learner is interested enough in what is going on to pay close attention. That is why play contexts are so much more efficient than traditional classrooms. (p. 12)

In earlier research on play at one center, Corsaro (1979) discovered that play episodes were often initiated by a request for acknowledgment of friendship. A familiar form was, "We're friends, right?" We learned that this interrogative with its tag question "right?" was generally acknowledged by an agreeing respondent's "Right!" Should the initiating child fail to receive an acknowledgment, one could expect the question to be repeated in some form. Similarly, we saw that introduction of new play themes required what Cook-Gumperz (1978) has called a "warrant" for play; that is, new themes must be negotiated.

Once we had noticed these seemingly simple strategies, we began to hear them throughout the day. Knowing what was necessary in order for children to establish or vary their social events, we could intervene and make suggestions more appropriately. We could more effectively support children in maintaining their often fragile interactions. When we learned that seemingly unimportant utterances provided the means for children to achieve their interactive goals, we could be attentive to breaches in discourse and help children clarify and focus their play intentions.

We also learned what elements of children's social knowledge were stable over time (such as their understanding of domestic roles). By using children's talk we could classify play episodes according to their themes and topics. When contrasted along these thematic dimensions we saw in very specific terms the ways that the play ecologies influenced and shaped interactive events. We could also see how children's understanding of the implied expectations of various settings were used by them to produce social behavior.

Central to the study was the notion that the context for play is dynamic, not just a static environmental "envelope" or "stimulus" for events. When an activity is negotiated communicatively, the activity then serves as a framing or shaping device that limits interpretation. This notion of context is derived from sociolinguists' work in the analysis of everyday communicative events like conversations, job interviews, or counseling sessions (Cook-Gumperz & Gumperz, 1982). In such research, context is seen as "understood" or "implied" rather than necessarily overt in communication. This understanding enables interactants to guide and maintain discourse with others. Knowing how contextual features intersect allows us to interpret, explain, and make predictions about the communicative situation.

Once the children agree to a play activity such as police and robbers, the activity itself frames the possible use and interpretation of the ensuing speech, gesture, and movements of the participants. By signaling context, either nonverbally or verbally (as in, "We're policemen, right?"), the context and its implications are made available to all participants as a shared cognitive construct, providing guidelines for further action and limiting the range of possibilities. To take the role of both a robber and a policeman, as one child had suggested, would represent a breach of social and ecological expectations. Any interaction in such a context would remain unfocused or falter unless a way could be discovered of incorporating the role of being both robber and policeman. Role boundaries could not be maintained, and the chase and capture sequences common to such play could not successfully ensue. "Who" would catch whom?"

On the other hand, the outcome of violations of such implied expectations sometimes results in marvelous new social transformations, especially as children's communicative ability matures. The cracker-stealing anecdote at the beginning of this chapter is an example of a playful attempt to achieve such a social transformation at an ecological level by trying to integrate the play expectations drawn from one area into that of another — the classroom. This group of 4½-year-olds playfully used their advancing cognitive, linguistic, and communicative ability to test the "elasticity" of the school's implied expectations and ecological boundaries.

One of the ways that play motivates language learning and the development of communicative competence comes from the potential demand that is inherent in its negotiation with others (Schank & Abelson, 1977). In the present study, negotiations of play schemes were seen as dynamic events often entailing theme expansion or elaboration. These were a major source of variation in the sociodramatic play episodes observed and recorded in the play yard study.

SOME OBSERVATIONS FROM THE SECOND STUDY: THREE EPISODES

Each of the following episodes occurred at a small sand table equipped with miscellaneous kitchen toys. It is located in an area of the play yard near the classroom. The first, "Basic Cooking," was chosen because it illustrates a basic scenario for the kinds of sociodramatic play episodes that teachers expect to see there. The second and third examples parallel the first but each involves unique thematic modifications and expansions of the basic scenario.

"basic cooking"

INITIATION. The following are excerpts from a transcript of a typical domestic role play. It underwent several transformations or theme expansions as the children negotiated their understanding of what was being played, determined who was participating, and sequenced their activities. This play occurred during the second month of nursery school and involved two previously unacquainted girls, Julianna (3 years, 1 month) and Dolores (3 years, 3 months). The taped duration of the play episode was 27 minutes, and it was still in progress when videotaping for the day ended. It shows how the teacher and ecological features of the area provide support for the play.

This episode reflected a sophisticated grasp of role-playing, initiated by the typical device of calling on friendship (Corsaro, 1979). The girls entered the same table area simultaneously to join several other children playing there. However, it soon became apparent that they were playing together.

Typically sociodramatic episodes for this area involved a sequence of three phases: (1) initiation, (2) negotiation, and (3) enactment. The first phase involved establishing a warrant for play and, in this case, "who" is to play (Cook-Gumperz, 1978).

> DOLORES. I'm your friend, okay? (*Dolores comes back to her first spot at sand table.*) I'm your friend, okay, Jul?
> JULIANNA. What? (*Julianna and Dolores continue "cooking," getting containers off the shelves, scooping sand into them, etc.*)
> DOLORES. I'm your friend.
> JULIANNA. You're not my friend?
> DOLORES. Yes, I am.

NEGOTIATION. The second phase of their play consisted of a lengthy negotiation of features of the warrant for play. They devoted much time to achieving an understanding about what they would make. The teacher intervened actively during this phase, usually making clarification requests about what was being made by the respective participants. Her purpose was to help the girls establish linguistically some shared theme and to model interactive strategies for them. Finally, Dolores pointedly indicated to Julianna that there was a task to be done jointly when she announced, "Julianna, we gotta do some work." She then went on to declare several times that she was "making soup." The teacher continued to intervene frequently, attempting to assist with the common understanding of what was being cooked by each of them. The following excerpt illustrates the difficulty of establishing a cohesive theme.

DOLORES. This is soup.

JULIANNA. I'm making . . .

DOLORES. No this . . . for us? . . . This is instant peanut butter. . . . I'm making peanut butter too. . . . This is peanut butter. Is that peanut butter?

JULIANNA. I'm making . . . water.

DOLORES. I'm making . . . I'm making . . . Julianna, we gotta do some work.
(Julianna and Dolores pretend to "cook." Dolores lifts a bowl toward Teacher.)

TEACHER. Do I want to taste it? Sure. *(Teacher gets a spoon and pretends to eat.)*

DOLORES. It's a soup.

TEACHER. Umm, that's good soup, Dolores.
(Julianna starts moving containers of sand onto the small table. Dolores keeps on "cooking.")

DOLORES. I don't need all this food. I can't eat all this food. Cause this is . . . this is . . . cause that's a soup. *(Dolores continues "cooking" at the sand table.)*

TEACHER. Soup.

DOLORES. This is . . . soup. . . . Julianna.

JULIANNA. What?

During this lengthy negotiation phase the girls did not verbally affirm that they were engaged in a coordinated cooking project or were making the same thing. Dolores's invitation to the teacher to "taste" her "soup" seems off topic in the light of subsequent events. No acknowledgment of soup making is elicited from Julianna, and Dolores immediately begins to direct Julianna in the table-setting sequence. Whether there was an implicit understanding about a shared theme in this play is unclear. However, such understanding could be inferred from the girls' synchronous movements, the use of similar toys, and the coordination of the activity of the two participants.

JULIANNA.   Should I put it right here? *(Julianna returns to small
   table with some plates and places them near Dolores.)*
DOLORES.   No, right there. *(Dolores points.)*
JULIANNA.   Right there? *(Julianna places the plates on the table.)*

ENACTMENT.   It is unclear from the transcript whether both children
had an awareness of what was to be enacted. It was never introduced
or acknowledged verbally, until Julianna started singing "Happy
Birthday" to Dolores, who hesitated a moment and then joined in.
Julianna then announced, "This is your birthday cake," and requested
that Dolores "blow out the candles." She repeated the request three
times, received no acknowledgment, and blew them out herself.
Despite this seeming rupture, the enactment of the party proceeded in
a fairly cohesive manner. Julianna later attempted to expand the
theme of the interaction to include wine for each of them and again
failed to get an acknowledgment on this detail from Dolores.

*(Julianna returns with another utensil. She walks around the
table with it, then returns to her place.)*
JULIANNA *(starts singing)*. Happy birthday to you, happy birthday to
   you.
DOLORES *(joins in)*. Happy birthday to you, happy birthday to you.
JULIANNA and DOLORES.   Happy . . . *(They stop singing.)*
JULIANNA *(to Dolores)*. This is your birthday cake. Blow out the
   candles.
   (Dolores goes back to wiping. Michael walks over to watch.)
JULIANNA.   Blow out the candles. *(Julianna points to something
   she holds upright in a pot of sand.)* Blow out the candles.
   *(Dolores mumbles something. Julianna blows out the candles
   herself.)*
JULIANNA *(cuts the cake)*. That's yours. . . . Want some cake? Some
   cake? *(Julianna takes a scoop out and walks around the side
   of the table to put some on Dolores's plate.)* Here's some cake
   for you.
DOLORES *(to Michael)*. Here's some cake for you. *(Dolores gestures to
   Michael to take the cake.)*
JULIANNA.   Let's get some cake.
   *(Michael walks away. Dolores brings another scoop around
   the table and puts it on another plate; she starts scooping her
   own.)*
JULIANNA *(runs back to the "cake")*. No, that isn't cake for you.
DOLORES.   I don't want no cake. *(Dolores takes the scoop from
   Julianna and serves more.)* That is a cake. That is a cake. That
   is a cake.
   *(Dolores mumbles as she scoops sand from the sand table
   into a container on the small table.)*

JULIANNA.   This is one for you. *(Julianna sets a wine glass at Dolores's place at the table.)* Here, take. Here, take this. *(Julianna "cuts" something and hands Dolores a plate while getting up.)* Here, take this.

DOLORES *(gets to the other side of the table, then hands something to Julianna)*. Cake. Here's your cake. Cake. Here's your cake.

WHAT WE LEARNED FROM "BASIC COOKING." This episode was representative of many that occurred at the small sand table. In it the children stayed well within the expectations of the ecology and verbally and nonverbally elaborated the theme as necessary to advance and maintain their play. Surprisingly, the birthday party, a major feature of the enactment, seemed not to have been verbally marked or negotiated by the participants.

Because of religious beliefs, Dolores's family had asked that she not celebrate her own birthday or participate in such occasions at school. The family also did not use alcoholic beverages. It appears that Dolores subtly avoided *verbal expression* of her participation in some aspects of the birthday party simply by participating at an activity level only; that is, she cut and served cake and began singing only after Julianna began to do so, and she failed to acknowledge the wine. By this means she avoided a breach in the interaction with Julianna but at the same time conformed to her family's sanctions. Further evidence for this interpretation was found in her failure to respond at several other critical junctures in theme progression. This suggested her silence was not accidental and under the circumstances demonstrated her communicative competence.

This episode resembled play whose function has been called "practice" or "role rehearsal." Nevertheless, it was not ritualistically performed and, despite the fact that the play appeared to be somewhat static, close examination showed that subtle communicative tasks were adroitly managed.

Two other episodes occurring at this same site, involving the same basic scenario, illustrated other efforts to articulate ideas socially. Each of these episodes, on the surface at least, seemed to reflect one of the traditional notions of role rehearsal or practice of social roles as the function of children's play.

"playing dead"

In this episode, Vanessa (4 years, 9 months) took the occasion of an unusual ecological variation (the addition of red food coloring to the available water) to introduce and attempt to establish socially a theme involving an egocentric interest in death and killing by poisoning. Her efforts had only modest success, despite her persuasiveness and verbal sophistication. Because she attempted to adapt the theme of killing by poisoning to the context of standard expectations for play at the sand table — that is, to the "local knowledge" of participants — she was partially successful in establishing her play theme with the other players. The social and ecological expectations implicit in the play theme necessitated that Vanessa's contributions be relevant. These expectations constituted an unseen curriculum for the play.

In the following segment of this interactive episode, Vanessa failed, despite using all her persuasive powers, to establish the theme of preparing poison cakes to "kill people." She was involved with three children, Caitlin (4 years, 6 months), Michael (4 years, 2 months), and William (4 years, 6 months). She succeeded in enlisting the participation of William, but Caitlin and Michael were more intent on killing "bad guys," more commonplace play yard adversaries. In this they stayed within the local expectations of the play yard about who could be "killed." Caitlin's reservations about the emerging theme were expressed when she said, "We don't want — I think I'm not playing." Vanessa then attempted to justify her idea of who could be killed by saying repeatedly, "You can *kill* the people who kill." However, not until Vanessa modified her assertion to "We can kill *monsters*" did she obtain an agreement from Caitlin. In substituting "monsters" for "people who kill," Vanessa adapted the identity of the victim to the expectations of the play yard. The following is the initiation and a part of the negotiation of this episode.

VANESSA. William, you gotta make a poison cake like I am.
CAITLIN *(stands opposite Vanessa)*. For God's sake, I'm gonna take all the water that we need.
WILLIAM *(stands to the left of Vanessa)*. *You* make a poison cake.
VANESSA. We gotta make two, one from you and one from me, and you're not making one.
WILLIAM. All *right*, I'll make them one. Mine will be many, mine will be poison cakes.
VANESSA. Yeh, then you can make many poison cakes.
WILLIAM. We have to make them be all over.
CAITLIN. We're gonna kill all the bad guys . . .
VANESSA. And we're gonna, and we're gonna kill . . .
CAITLIN. We don't want . . . I think I'm not playing . . .
MICHAEL. What?
VANESSA. You can . . . You can *kill* the people who kill. You can *kill*

the people who kill. You can *kill* the people who kill. . . . We can kill the monsters.

CAITLIN.   Okay.

VANESSA.   Yeh, me and William are gonna kill the monsters.

MICHAEL.   We're gonna kill the bad guys, that's what we're gonna do.

Although the choice of theme may be determined at one level by affective necessity, realization is achieved through the social means of communicative strategies and knowledge of local context expectations. A major value of sociodramatic play for the child lies in its fundamental social nature. It creates conditions that require children to exercise their communicative skills to enlist others in it.

"monster cakes"

This episode demonstrated how new expectations were generated socially and became a part of the accustomed context for play. Here the children utilized theme elaboration and expansion to adapt an unusual event to the local knowledge and expectations not only of one but of three different ecological settings. A brief synopsis of this follows.

Play at the small sand table had been going on for about 20 minutes. It involved three children: Maurice (4 years, 9 months), Adam (4 years, 8 months), and Bradley (4 years, 1 month). The children were generally engaged in "cooking" together. The teacher had added food coloring to the water for the second day, and as a consequence there was considerable talk about making poison cakes. The initial segment of this episode began when Bradley entered the area and announced to all that he planned to make "poisonous soup." The original children were shortly joined by three others, Caitlin, Melanie, and Michael; but agreements were reached on what was to be made only among Bradley, Adam, and Maurice. Up to this point, the episode followed a pattern similar to many others that occurred in this area: (1) initiation, (2) negotiation of the cooking theme and who is playing, and 3) the presentation of the "food" or enactment of consumption. An important variation occurred in the invention of who would be the recipients for the "poisonous soup." They were to be "grouches" or "strangers," and they were to be adversely affected, not nourished, by their consumption of the food. This theme foreshadowed a conflict in appropriateness expectations for this area, as opposition to strangers or villains generally occurred in the large climbing area at the rear of the play yard, where monsters ranged freely or were opposed as necessary as a part of the children's accustomed expectations for that area. The necessity for a theme expansion was predictable.

The children transported and recycled the culmination of the episode to a more suitable location, namely, the deck that overlooked both the large sandpit and the large climber area, where child-initiated themes dominated. This move and consequent theme expansion were necessary because the "grouches" and "strangers" behaved in ways that violated the appropriateness expectations of the small sand table area, particularly at the end when the poisoned "grouches" began yelling and throwing sand, albeit in a linguistically well-coordinated and cohesive manner. Evidence that the children contextualized this move to appropriateness expectations from two differing areas came when (1) food was placed on a tablelike structure rather than on the ground, and (2) the two girls who joined the boys engaged in a very "domestic pretend" clean-up of the plates of the "poisonous food" recklessly spilled by the "strangers" a second time. Such behavior appeared to integrate play schemes derived from the small sand table into the large sandpit. When the teacher asked the children to clean up the "mess" that the "strangers" had made in spilling the cakes, they gave further evidence of their awareness of the specific appropriateness expectations of the area they had entered. Maurice and Bradley, in a gleeful parody, began to pretend they were engaged in constructive play by using shovels to spread the sand that had been spilled about by the "grouches."

The children successfully maintained interactive cohesion in this episode primarily because the thematic variation and its consequent contextualization drew upon their shared knowledge of local expectations. The mechanisms employed in these theme expansions suggest that transformation in symbolic play arises not only by chance, environmental stimuli, or personal necessity, but also from social motivation.

what we learned about the children

In the episodes that were selected for analysis, we found that children recognized that the topics that they wished to insert in discourse had to be relevant to the ongoing script or theme (Corsaro, 1985). We learned that, when theme expansions were related to shared understanding of appropriateness expectations for play events and setting, interactive cohesion was more readily maintained. In the episode in which one child's personal and subjective interest in death was introduced, a greater difficulty in integration of theme to context was encountered.

The study suggested that interactive cohesion is often dependent upon the ecological features of settings; however, when an unusual event occurs children marshal their interactive skills to articulate and expand the thematic content of their role play to accommodate to the event. To illustrate this point, in the episode called "Monster Cakes," Bradley had difficulty in repeated attempts to negotiate putting cakes on the ground to be eaten in a "monstrous" way. Humming the theme from a well-known television program, "Batman," and rotating his arms in a "walking" fashion, Bradley subtly signaled a new location for their play. By this imaginative means he utilized his knowledge of context and interactive skills to lead the play participants to a more suitable site for the reenactment of this play.

Children use three forms of knowledge to negotiate their own scenarios. The first involves scriptlike conventional sources of social knowledge (Garvey, 1977; Nelson & Gruendal, 1979) and is exemplified by interchanges such as "You're my friend. Right?" Second, children use environmentally defined knowledge such as how one behaves at the sand table. Third, the specific histories of their own interactions are a source of particular social knowledge. Caitlin, William, and Vanessa may bring their monster cake into subsequent scenarios. All three forms of knowledge provide children with motivation for the continuation of a particular play interaction.

what we learned about intervention

The study provided specific evidence for the potential of play for learning and demonstrated how it reveals its hidden curriculum and provides important opportunities for creative evolution of the school's curriculum for socialization. By knowing that the contexts for play are dynamic, teachers became much more alert to the emergence and elaboration of children's play themes. Knowledge of who initiates and how negotiations are conducted enables the teacher to identify children who have a stake in a given play episode. This can be important when the teacher attempts to bring focus or to sustain an interaction in a relevant way. Collaborative play and "sharing" then make sense in terms of what children are trying to do as they communicate. For example, having a grasp of who was involved in playing robbers and policemen enabled the teacher to solicit assistance from the children themselves in considering the ramifications of being both a robber and a policeman. The dilemma was resolved and cohesion maintained when the teacher suggested that the participants alternate roles.

From my research I had obtained information on how children handle potentially conflicting features of their interactions themselves. Participants acknowledge their understanding and agreement regarding introducing and expanding play themes. Children need to know appropriate communicative strategies for accomplishing this. Agreements about negotiation of themes has to be signaled, if only by a "right?" and a "Right!"

In my study, theme expansion generally marked the insertion of new material. These moments were often fragile ones, such as when teachers introduced food coloring in the water at the domestic kitchen play area. Following this event children were no longer just "cooking"; they were making "poisonous cakes" and needed to deal with what proceeded from their imaginative expansion of the "cooking" theme. Their invention of appropriate recipients for "poisonous" food culminated in a violation of expectations for play at a domestic play area. The teacher had inadvertently set up a challenging social problem for children to solve. They could no longer rely upon a ritualistic recycling of well-known themes of "cooking" and having a "party." Analysis of the interactive episodes also revealed the use of variations in speech or register of voice to signal roles. Communicative strategies vary culturally, and children at play in integrated nursery schools may be required to be bidialectical. Pitch, stress, intonation, and rhythm all play a part in communicating meaning and intent. Nonverbal cues such as gesture, manipulation of objects, and physical movement also operate as co-occurring elements.

The cohesiveness of interactions was ascertained by the synchrony or asynchrony of these co-occurring features. Was the "loner" in or out of "sync?" Was her play parallel or interactive? In this way the points of least cohesiveness in interaction could also be ascertained. Knowing that children must coordinate these co-occurring elements suggested questions we might ask when a play episode faltered or a child had difficulty entering into play with others. Has one interactant failed to acknowledge her participation in or understanding of an important aspect of theme in the ongoing discourse event? Is she attempting to insert material that is off the topic? Does her contribution need to be negotiated?

Rather than simply asking interactants to "share" or "cooperate" with a potential participant whose possibly irrelevant overtures have been rejected, we might propose that the newcomer play nearby at a similar activity. Here she may become more attentive to the needs of the interaction, discover what is being played, and possibly consider a contribution she might make. Often asking the established pair or group to share a small part of their toys with the newcomer in a parallel but separate space reassures them that *their* interactive space will not be violated. This gives time for possible points of intersection with the newcomer to be safely considered without danger to the fragile interaction that has already been established.

In these ways our efforts to help became more relevant because they addressed the social needs of interactants, resulting in the emergence of a richer and more dynamic curriculum for socialization. We began seeing children's play as a complex dance with its own logic, rather than a game of Ping-Pong. As we studied children's efforts to interact and integrate their play themes into the play context, processes by which the child's world is constructed through play and language were revealed to us.

VIEWING PLAY FROM A NEW STANCE

Videotaped observations of play episodes are increasingly available in nursery schools. Whether or not they are available, the understanding of what is being accomplished by children in play recommends that teachers observe play from a new stance. This new stance includes knowledge of the ways that social and ecological factors combine to create sets for children's play.

A deeper analysis of children's interactions during play allows teachers to notice children's use of conventional social exchanges in negotiating roles, expectations for play shaped by the physical environment, and personal histories of the co-players as they maintain and expand play themes. This knowledge makes for more effective intervention in setting the stage for play and in guiding its course. Intervention in play becomes specific to its context. With this knowledge teachers can better support children's efforts to achieve social identity as they construct their social world. Teachers can illuminate theory about the functions of play rather than blindly invoke it. With empirical evidence, they can trust the validity of some of their intuitions about the worth of play and make judgments and evaluations that further the processes of understanding and change.

6
extending the bridge

Chapter 2 considered both traditional and current views of the function of children's play, setting out in relief some aspects of the literature on theory and practice about play that were ambiguous or raised questions. In our research we addressed some of these ambiguities and questions for ourselves. Van Hoorn considered the function of parent-infant play and how that context serves specific cultural as well as developmental needs. Monighan-Nourot examined the traditional paradigms for looking at play stages, attempting to clarify for herself the role of solitary play. Scales adapted methods derived from ethnography to look at play as it occurred in her setting, noting the subtle ways that social and ecological cues for behavior influence play in the preschool.

Initiating our own research forced us to become familiar with the work of other play researchers, examine historical antecedents to current theories about play, and acquaint ourselves with accepted research methodologies. We had to formulate our questions and develop systematic and verifiable procedures to investigate them. The research that each of us conducted allowed us to reflect on our practice and changed how we subsequently came to support and describe play in our own programs. We found that the answers to our questions were not final but led to other questions that encouraged us to elaborate our knowledge of play and development along both practical and theoretical dimensions.

NEW VIEWS FROM THE BRIDGE

As each teacher-researcher resolved her questions and reshaped her view of play in her own classroom, another process emerged as well. Reaching the summit of one's expectations, so to speak, allows one a new vista to contemplate. As each research question was resolved, new sets of practical dilemmas and/or theoretical views were revealed.

Van Hoorn answered many of her questions about infant-parent games, such as how and when they happen and what their features are. The question of goal setting for a parent-generated curriculum and the question of how to define learning remained. She did not find the cognitive features that she had anticipated in the games. As later reflection underscored the importance of their interpersonal features, she became interested in the ways that games contribute to the development of communication within the family and the infant's social-cognitive skills. The "cultural curriculum" that emerged from her work sets the stage for provocative speculation about the ways that early childhood educators can adapt curricula based on play to individual needs of children.

Monighan-Nourot structured her environment so that solitary players might have the freedom to choose to play away from the group. She did this both in terms of space and in training the adults to honor children's needs for privacy. In doing so she created new issues: How can we define the spaces for private and group play, where do we draw the line if a conflict occurs, and how can we give the adults something to do other than to encourage group social interaction and sharing of materials? She had to make a concerted effort to train the participating parents to become involved in children's play in ways other than spectatorship of its group dynamics, and to determine when intervention was appropriate and when it seemed wiser to observe and receive information from the children.

Scales's study resulted in a preschool environment that so effectively supported peer play that one solitary player wondered about his place in the scheme of the setting:

> The teacher observes Richard playing by himself, and then wandering from one activity to another. He appears to be at "loose ends" and she wonders why he is not playing with his close friend Gregory. She suggests, "Why don't you play with Gregory? I see him over there in the sandbox." Richard answers her with a

pleading look on his face, "Do you think it would be okay just for me to play by myself today?"

Scales and her staff then began to devise means for supporting solitary players in a social environment.

As each of us "crossed" to the other side of the gap between teacher and researcher, a new view emerged for us to consider. The resolution of some of the original questions and the unveiling of new facets also shed new light on developmental theory as it relates to play, and on teachers' roles in contributing to its expansion and refinement.

PLAY AS A BRIDGE TO PRACTICE

In addressing the practical implications of our research, we are struck by two factors illuminated in all of our studies: the relationship between home and school and the use of play in assessment of cognitive, social, and emotional development of young children.

linking home and school

In studying the relationship between home and school, we explored the significance of the fact that an increasing number of very young children are cared for outside their homes for many of their waking hours.

As Van Hoorn's study implies, play between parent and child sets the stage for an atmosphere of trust thought by many educators and developmental psychologists to influence the lifelong development of self-esteem and social relationships. Recent research links social competence in the preschool years to early trust in the caregiver-infant relationship (Clarke-Stewart & Hevey, 1981; Sroufe, 1979; Sroufe & Waters, 1977; Waters, Wippman & Sroufe, 1979.) This suggests that the effective reciprocity established through play influences a child's ability to establish boundaries of private and social experience as he develops.

Assuming that the parents in Van Hoorn's study are like most parents, educators can encourage them to follow their own natural inclinations in playing with their children when they do spend time with them. Whether parents work outside the home or not, it is important that they feel confident about the quality of their interactions with their children. The proliferation of didactic materials for parents to use in teaching their children cognitive skills brings an increased need for educators to explain why they might better spend time sharing the pleasures of play with their children.

Van Hoorn's study was initiated in response to a need for a culturally relevant child-centered curriculum for *home-based* programs. However, educators addressing needs of families of diverse economic and cultural backgrounds in childcare settings may find this "natural" curriculum both the most developmentally sound and the easiest to implement. It follows that a thorough understanding of the features that distinguish play of various cultures will be a goal of sensitive teachers using such curriculum in their settings. (See Sutton-Smith & Heath, 1981, and Schwartzman, 1984, for an elaboration of this idea.)

If parent-infant play is well designed to support the multiple needs of babies, then a play-based curriculum for their caregivers is in order. Research indicates that by as early as 6 to 8 weeks of age infants have begun to differentiate their interaction patterns with several caregivers (Brazelton, 1982). Such curricula can serve the development of trusting and flexible relationships with caregivers outside the home as well as within the family.

Our work with preschoolers illuminates the relativity of values and styles of play at school and at home. Parental attitudes toward make-believe and toward work and play, as well as the concrete experiences children bring from their cultural and/or religious backgrounds, surface in play at school (Curry & Arnaud, 1984).

The insights gained by teachers into both individual children and home environments may be garnered as tools by which to understand play and to intervene in it with sensitivity. For example, the child who watches too many cartoons and the child who is stressed by divorce offer cues in their play to their teachers. The child whose family discourages birthday celebrations and the child whose "play" at home consists of alphabet-recognition games also reveal themselves to the sensitive observer of play. Children who come from homes that represent alternatives to traditional nuclear families may show differing play patterns. For example, the research of Monighan (1986) and others (Di Pietro, 1981; Forys & McCune-Nicholich, 1984; Joopnarine & Mounts, 1985; Langlois & Downs, 1980; Tizard & Hughes, 1984) indicates that fathers engage in rough-and-tumble play with both sons and daughters, while mothers play more verbal games. What might be the implications of this for children who live in single-parent homes? The observation of children's spontaneous activity in play offers teachers a unique opportunity to assess it and, if necessary, to intervene in it or to use observations to advise parents.

Many teachers face these issues concerning links between home and school. Many doubt that they can clarify the value of play in the classroom for parents whose only expressed concerns are for their children's academic success. Many teachers are so frustrated by the pressures to "jump start" preschoolers that they feel they can do nothing to justify play in their curriculum.

using play to assess and support development

Much of the literature on social development in early childhood and a growing body of research on cognitive development in early childhood settings draws on play as both a source of information for assessing development and as a context for fostering development (Bretherton, 1984; Fein & Rivkin, 1986; Yawkey & Pellegrini, 1984).

Special educators who work with young handicapped children have long used research tools to measure the effectiveness of their techniques for teaching skills and modifying behavior. Studies of group process have been less common. A good example of the potential effectiveness of assessment and appropriate intervention may be found in two teachers' work with a classroom of preschool deaf children who were being mainstreamed into a public-school kindergarten. The deaf children's teacher used sociometric techniques and photographed observations of play to see how the integration was proceeding during the first weeks of joint class activities. She and the public-school teacher discovered that the deaf children nominated only other deaf children as their favorite playmates. They played only with deaf children and clustered together during large group sessions. The same pattern held for the original kindergarten group.

Both teachers were dismayed to find so little evidence of integration. They decided to make "signing" the focus of the curriculum for the next month. Children in both groups practiced in sign language useful phrases and the names of objects. At the end of 3 weeks the systematic observations the teachers made revealed a dramatic change. Children from both groups claimed "best friends" in the other group, and photographs of their play showed them smiling, signing, and interacting. Both teachers are continuing play observations to enhance their understanding of individual children and the group dynamics of the classroom.

What, specifically, do teachers of young children need to know about their play in order to assess and support development effectively? They need to know what to expect of children of varying ages as they play in group settings. Teachers also need information about how such factors as the number of children in the group and their ages affect how closely children conform to developmental norms. For example, to allow for solitary play in a mixed-aged group, the environment may be structured differently than in a single-age group. As Scales's work implies, the housekeeping corner provides a familiar anchor for the play of some children, while more unstructured contexts challenge the imaginations of others. The teacher needs to understand how to balance requirements for social and private experiences, both for young children who spend most of their waking hours in groups and for the only child whose contact with other children is limited to the time at school.

The teacher needs to understand the ways that play supports the development of symbolic skills needed to read and learn to use numbers. Perhaps he can convince a parent that the symbolic transformation evident in pretending that a block is a ham sandwich or a fire truck contributes to the understanding that combinations of shapes and lines represent sounds and words of spoken language. The teacher needs to understand the ways that children come to represent and coordinate the perspectives of others in their play. Such knowledge can justify the purchase of several sets of identical play props for 2-year-olds who are not yet ready to share, or explain why realistic replicas of food might be a poor choice for the 5-year-olds.

It is a large order indeed for teachers of young children to honor the needs of individual children, and of the group, as well as the families they serve. Where can teachers go to get information regarding these concerns? Will each teacher's questions be answered, or will others even ask the same questions? There clearly is a great need for more coordinated efforts to generate and share information.

PLAY AS A BRIDGE TO THEORY

Closely related to the pursuit of solutions to problems encountered by teachers in their practice is the structure of play from the perspective of developmental theory. From that perspective, a common assumption runs as a major thread in the analysis of our research in play: Private and social forms of psychological functioning reflect two sides of the same coin. An extension of this idea is our belief that play during early childhood demonstrates development in both private and social forms of symbolic expression.

Two questions arise from these assumptions. The first is, What is the nature of the "core" common to the modes of private and social functioning? The second is, What is the developmental process that results in the changes in play we and others have observed with young children?

the common core of private and social functioning

As we look at the recent research and theory related to children's play and note teachers' descriptions of the growing sophistication in play they observe in children, the theme of symbolic "distancing" emerges often. "Distancing" describes the degree to which one uses mental representation and imagination to formulate ideas that are different from the object or context itself (Sigel, 1982). Distancing can be seen in two major ways. One is the distance between self and other that we see in children's ability to consider the perspectives of others in their play and in their communication within and about play (Fein, 1984). Children whose play shows distance in this respect are able to consider the roles they play in relation to others and are able to shift back and forth between expression that is "in" the play and expression that is "about" the play. For example, 5-year-old Sally skillfully discusses the space cat and her fellow astronauts as part of her role as captain of a spacecraft. Along with this we can see her also shift "out" of her role as actress in the play to that of director of the play. She says to a prospective player who is bidding to join their drama, "Well, I guess you could be another cat, or a dog, even; we already have all the people. . . . " Then, with tacit or active agreement from her co-actors, she assigns the new player to his "bed" in the spaceship and returns to her role as captain. This kind of distancing calls upon complex symbolic skills as she shifts her own role from captain to director and manages those of other players within the shared context of the drama being played out.

A second kind of distancing is one major focus of research in play: representational distancing in the objects and gestures children use as symbols for the props for their play. The child who cries because he does not have an exact replica of a walkie-talkie to use is less competent with this kind of distancing than the child who appropriates a wooden block when all the toy walkie-talkies are in use. This type of distancing is also seen when children abstract the features of roles and situations in order to apply them in a new context. In Scales's study the boys who stealthily pilfered crackers from the snack table and moved them to a new place were acting out their representation of the role of thieves as well as the "rules" implicit in the snack table situation.

The first kind of distancing describes the child's differentiation of self from others, and the second describes her progression from concrete to abstract symbols to signify meaning. Their common core in development is the ability to step out of the self or the present context and entertain a new perspective.

As Monighan-Nourot's and Scales's work illustrates, mastering the cognitive skill of distancing enables children eventually to discriminate situations in which private and social forms of communication and play are appropriate. Children first learn to discriminate the features of solitary or group functioning. They then begin to experiment with moving between private and social modes of playing, and finally they learn to consider the perspectives of others by communicating their intentions. So, when Frank recognizes that Mauricio's efforts to share his box of Leggos mean that Mauricio doesn't know that Frank wants to play alone, Frank learns to say, "I really want to do this myself now."

developmental processes in children's play

If we assume that distancing describes the symbolic skill reflected in both cognitive representation and social negotiation, we are still left with the task of describing the developmental process underlying the emergence of these skills. Drawing on our study of theory and research in human development, we assume that the process is one of differentiation and reintegration. In analyzing our own research at three stages of child development, we have documented three aspects: contextualization, decontextualization, and recontextualization.

CONTEXTUALIZATION. In reviewing Van Hoorn's work we infer that the perspectives of self and other are merged. In infancy the differentiation we described as social distancing has not yet occurred. Parent and child contextualize play within their relationship. The child learns that "this is play; this is fun; this feels good to us both." Even the play that will later become competitive, the "chaser-chasee" games of infancy, have no winner and loser. Both players are winners, as the common goal of shared excitement is reached. Within this shared context, then, begins the process of decontextualization. Mutuality of affect and activity expands to reciprocal turn taking; the parent claps and smiles, saying, "Pat-a-cake, pat-a-cake, baker man," and the child responds with a smile, clapping and making sounds spoken in rhythm with the rhyme. The hider becomes the seeker, then the seeker becomes the hider. The easily flowing transformations to new roles or contexts and the return to the original are orchestrated by the parent within the secure context of mutual enjoyment. Infant and parent are merged, as are private and social contexts. As the infant's play becomes more differentiated, object play is facilitated by the parent. The child more often uses physical objects as the parent models them and encourages both mental representation of objects (peek-a-boo) and symbolic representation ("Tortillitas"; This Little Piggy).

DECONTEXTUALIZATION. This process is most clearly illustrated in Monighan-Nourot's description of the 3-year-olds in her sample. Cognitive distancing is most evident in their solitary play. They engage in elaborated make-believe with toy vehicles or household props. They also enjoy social events with peers: Running, jumping, and leaping are common shared activities. Rarely do they combine the distancing required by mutuality and reciprocity with the distancing required to use objects symbolically in pretend play. Both kinds of distancing are present in their repertoires, but contextualization still prevails as a secure base for using skill in distancing: The self or a familiar peer or sibling supports distancing with objects. The easy pleasure of sensorimotor activity supports the distancing required for coordinating the perspective of fellow players. Ritualized games such as follow-the-leader and Farmer in the Dell provide this support, and such activity, repeated in ritual forms, offers a bridge to the symbolic extension and coordination of roles that evolve as children play games in more sophisticated ways.

As the preschooler develops, the efforts to differentiate perspectives of self and others and to differentiate features of objects, roles, and situations come more easily. Children become increasingly able to combine the symbolic distancing of objects with the social distancing required of the group dramatic player. Along with this comes the beginning understanding of the implicit rules of private and social contexts and the kinds of communication needed to operate effectively in each. The preschooler experiments with the features of private and social contexts through parallel play and collective monologue. Awareness of others' perspectives comes from the conflict that arises when the group player impinges on a solitary context or vice-versa; features of communication with the self and communication with others become decontextualized and represented.

RECONTEXTUALIZATION. This process is best illustrated by Scales's work. Here older preschoolers return to the state shared by the infant and parent described by Van Hoorn, where "play is pleasing to both of us." There is a mutual enjoyment arising from merged perspectives, but recontextualization involves conscious perspective taking on the part of the child. Once she has separated the perspectives of self and others and represented them, those perspectives may be "recontextualized" to create mutual enjoyment for all the players. This is the level of sophistication that we see when children make concessions and select alternatives that will please others; such pleasing of others insures that the play will continue: "If I please you, then you will play with me." By this time, children also find ways to bring into the group context themes they might have previously played in solitary contexts. The child who has a private need to bring in a death theme manages to negotiate the "fit" of this into the stream of group play, simultaneously meeting her need for a private theme and a social context. The discrimination of private and social perspectives and their contexts is now reintegrated at a more complex level, in the attempt to "have your cake and eat it too." (Isn't that what we all try to do when we play?)

IMPLICATIONS FOR INTERVENING IN PLAY

We have now discussed the new questions that were raised as our initial questions were resolved through research. Discovering one facet of play led us to see new ones embedded in our new perspective. We have also talked about how theoretical paradigms of play were empirically grounded in our observations of children and our analyses of what we found. The third step is to draw implications for practice in the classroom, based on our view of the features of early childhood play and the processes that are reflected and supported in its development.

How do we know as teachers which situations call for a particular perspective on children's play? At times the most sensitive intervention is based on looking outward from the facets of play to consider children's personality differences or families' cultural values. At other times looking inward from the facets of play to examine the structure of play helps us to intervene most appropriately. Play helps us to understand a child's capacity for representing objects symbolically, and it illuminates our knowledge of a child's ability to coordinate his perspective with those of other children.

Teachers need to consider several questions when intervening in children's play. These questions fall into the categories of *how, when,* and *why.*

how shall we intervene?

The kinds of intervention a teacher may choose range along a continuum from passive to active. Observation of a child's use of props in solitary dramatic play marks a passive form of intervention, while drawing a child into a hospital play theme by asking her to play the role of the doctor encompasses a very active role for the teacher. Providing new props for play or rearranging the environment into more closed or open spaces constitutes a relatively passive intervention. Parallel play with gradual variation reciprocally imitated by child and teacher lies close to the passive pole. Questioning a child about her pretend or sensorimotor play is slightly more active. For example, the teacher might ask a child she sees with a doll in a stroller, "Are you taking your baby to the hospital?" Sliding into the child's play as a complementary actor would be more active than questioning but less so than directing the play. For example, a teacher might say, "You know, Jane, my baby had a cough that sounded just like that last week, and I took her to the doctor for some medicine." By intervening and using a "play" voice, the teacher is providing a cue for Jane to consider extending her theme to include a visit to the doctor and modeling the use of make-believe for her.

Intervention need not always occur within the play space. For example, the teachers in Scales's play yard noted that the children did not do much digging in the large sandpit. They then realized that the children's experiences of construction projects were limited, so they developed a play curriculum specifically for the sand area. Another way they might have followed up on this insight would have been to take an active role in extending the children's knowledge of construction projects. This was done in another preschool, where the teachers took small groups of children on weekly trips to view the site of a new freeway under construction. On each occasion, they photographed the progress being made, week by week, adding to their visual documentation. Not surprisingly, the children's block play reflected their interest in the freeway construction.

In another preschool, a visit to the small airport where one of the fathers worked as an airplane mechanic stimulated new play themes with the outdoor climbing equipment as well as the blocks.

In addition to field trips, invitations to adults in the community and parents to visit the children and demonstrate their work often turn out to be indirect interventions in children's play. So do the books and pictures that teachers highlight for the children, as well as the stories they tell them.

when shall we intervene?

The second question to consider when intervening in children's play is the timing. *When* is it appropriate to use any particular form of intervention? Even observing play may be intrusive when children are playing out themes that challenge adult authority. For example, when 4-year-olds have a secret hideout, the teacher may deliberately avoid intruding. Another consideration involves what Schwartzman (1976) calls "sideways glances" at children's play. If two assertive children who are often leaders in classroom play are battling it out over who gets to be captain of the pirate ship, the sensitive teacher observes inconspicuously and lets them resolve their conflict themselves. On the other hand, sometimes sophisticated players bully younger or less experienced players into situations that call for limit setting by the teacher. Knowledge of the history and social roles reflected in play themes and roles can be an important factor in deciding if and when to intervene.

A related consideration is balance. Sometimes children need to play for 3 weeks straight with the wooden train set and do little else during the day. Sometimes engaging in one kind of play (such as aggressive gun play) to the exclusion of other activities reflects a need for the teacher to intervene. Perhaps the child concerned doesn't know how to play in other ways, or perhaps his understanding of social and private roles is too limited to try anything new. The question of balance for that particular child is one that the sensitive teacher can address.

why intervene?

The last question we ask about intervention is, *Why* intervene? Does careful attention to the child's play have implications for the parents? What about parents who use their "play time" with their child to drill her on the ABC's? If this child comes to school with few make-believe skills, the teacher may want to help both the child and her parent discover make-believe play. Parents of infants can benefit from this kind of intervention as well. Teachers may model reciprocal games for parents of infants as alternatives to more structured materials and toys on the market today.

Concern also arises when a teacher sees changes or elements in the child's play at school that reflect a crisis in the home. The birth of a sibling or the death of a pet might cue the teacher to intervene. Even when stressful home situations are beyond the parent's immediate control or awareness, the teacher can intervene in ways that help the child to cope more effectively. An example of this is seen in Griffin's book, *Island of Childhood* (1982), where she presents case studies of children as they respond to their teacher's sensitive guidance of their play. Anecdotes or more detailed records from children's play provide powerful evidence when teachers are reporting children's progress to parents. They are essential in referring a child for special services.

Another reason to intervene involves getting information about the children. Will a simple change in play props or outdoor space change the social dynamic in the classroom or encourage groups to do different things? Sometimes the children request that a teacher intervene. Perhaps a group of girls wants to create a private place for their "club." A teacher can help them to do this without violating the rights of other children.

The last and perhaps most important reason for intervention in play is that of professional self-reflection by the teacher. The most stunning example of this process is offered by Paley in her book, *Boys and Girls: Superheroes in the Doll Corner* (1984). Paley courageously and eloquently describes her efforts to intervene in the play of the kindergartners she teachers. She confronts her biases about the differences she observes in the play of boys and girls at that age and explores alternative means of redirecting loud and conflictual play. Most significantly, she explores her own ways of coming to terms with the children's needs and her needs for acceptance and boundaries.

Such techniques of observation and professional self-reflection are useful with other issues that may "slip by" our awareness as teachers. One of these issues is coming to terms with our own personal biases about quiet and aggressive play and private and group symbolization (Sutton-Smith & Heath, 1981). Other issues include cooperation versus competition in play and the kinds of sexual or bodily-function language ("toilet talk") we observe in children's play. Observation in one's own classroom and reflection on one's self offer insights for improving one's practice as a teacher. At the same time they contribute to an empirically grounded research base in early childhood education.

Our research was based directly on the home and classroom observations we made. By seeking answers to questions that arose from our own practice as teachers, we encountered questions that others had asked about play and development. As we extended our research beyond our own settings, we accomplished two things: We enabled ourselves to gain information regarding our own questions, and, by adapting the constraints and methods of research, we each viewed a larger "slice" of the behaviors we chose to study. Such research controls and protocols forced each teacher to look be-yond her setting to see what she could find in the experiences of others that corroborated, contradicted, or supplemented her own view.

Such work, in effect, allowed each teacher-researcher to create an "extended family" viewpoint on her own practice. This process commonly goes on in educational settings as teachers informally discuss the questions and problems that arise in their own classrooms. When presenting research information to teachers in staff development or inservice education, we have often noticed the relief expressed by teachers that others face similar dilemmas. All of us can find comfort in the efforts made by others to pursue solutions, if not in the success of the solutions themselves. For us this was the beginning of building a bridge between the worlds of the teacher and the researcher.

CROSSING THE BRIDGE

So they began solemnly dancing round and round Alice, every now and then treading on her toes when they passed too close, and waving their fore-paws to mark the time, while the Mock Turtle sang this, very slowly and sadly: —

"Will you walk a little faster?" said a whiting to a snail,
"There's a porpoise close behind us, and he's treading on my tail.
See how eagerly the lobsters and the turtles all advance!
They are waiting on the shingle — will you come and join the dance?
  Will you, wo'n't you, will you, wo'n't you, will you join the dance?
  Will you, wo'n't you, will you, wo'n't you, wo'n't you join the dance?"

(Carroll, Alice in Wonderland, 1865/1946, p. 118)

In reflecting on our experiences as teachers who conducted research in our own settings, we have begun to see ourselves in a new role as teacher-researchers. Although each of us effected a transformation in role and thus in perspective from teacher to researcher, the experiences subsequent to completing our research have brought us full circle, back to the role of teacher. Yet, as we return to our teaching roles, the enrichment gained from the experience of a transformed perspective remains strong. New perspectives on our settings, the individuals we teach, the development and function of

play, and our own perceptions of ourselves as professionals have
changed our work as teachers.

Earlier in this chapter we related our changed perceptions
regarding our environments and the parents and children we work
with, and our expanded understanding of children's play. In this
section we explore the final and perhaps most important effect of
these transformations: reflection on our professional roles as early
childhood educators.

the nature of teaching

Teaching as art; teaching as science. Teaching as giving; teaching
as receiving. All of these aspects of our roles in the lives of children
and adults have come to the foreground during our reflective discussions. The teacher as both artist and scientist is a central notion in
the field of education. Good teachers as they practice are informed by
a background of science in such forms as developmental theory and
research, curriculum design, and objective evaluation. But it is the
creative synthesis of this knowledge base with the requirements of the
immediate situation that enable the teacher to act spontaneously and
appropriately in what some have called the "teachable moment."

Science reenters the foreground as teachers reflect on their
teachable moments with individuals or groups of children and use
their knowledge base to plan and predict what they will do the next
day or at the next opportunity for a similar teaching-learning
occasion. In such a manner, alternating between the creative "I" in the
moment and the evaluative "me" in reflection, teachers develop and
sustain their professional roles.

George Herbert Mead (1934) describes this process in his theory
of the development of a sense of self during early childhood. The
child acts spontaneously, in the moment, as "I" — the self as subject.
With growing experience in considering the perspectives of others,
children also develop the capacity to reflect on their behavior from
the viewpoints of others. They learn to "step outside" themselves
and regard the "me" as a social object. A third feature of Mead's theory
is the use of the reflective "me" as a means for planning and predicting subsequent interactions with other people. The more
sophisticated one's sense of self as social object (the "me"), the more
accurate and informed are subsequent plans to be executed in the
moment by the "I."

However, there is a catch here. An important element of the self as
subject (the "I") in experience is the capacity to act creatively and

spontaneously in response to others and a given situation. Thus, for the child, the most carefully memorized performance or planned project is subject to the internally generated messages from the "I." Perhaps a needed trip to the bathroom or an emo- tional response to a situation takes precedence in the actual behavior seen.

In *The Day Care Dilemma*, Blum (1983) describes a day in the life of Ivy Dennison, a 3-year-old who spends her weekdays at a daycare center. As Ivy arrives at the center, she occupies herself with a puzzle while she awaits her teacher's arrival:

> More teachers also begin to arrive and take their assigned children to their assigned rooms. When Jane, Ivy's teacher, comes in, Ivy gets up from her chair. "No," says Jane, "you need to finish that puzzle so someone else can use it." Ivy is afraid that if she spends too long on that puzzle, Jane will go to the 3-year-old class without her. She really wants to go with Jane. So she tries to hurry through the puzzle but can't get it right. She sees that Jane's attention is elsewhere, so she leaves the puzzle undone. She has a conflict between wanting to please Jane by obeying her and wanting to be with Jane. The need for the security of Jane's physical presence wins out. It is now 8:30 in the morning. (p. 36)

For the teacher, a similar process may occur. In reflecting on the "I" as teacher, he evaluates his previous performance and plans subsequent behavior. Yet the imagined situation and the one that actually takes place may be very different:

> The kindergarten teacher had carefully planned a discussion at circle time to follow up on the field trip to the "Pumpkin Patch" taken by the class the day before. She had samples of hay and pumpkins and was prepared to demonstrate how a jack-o-lantern was carved. All of a sudden, a fire truck came wailing up the street and stopped in view of the classroom windows. All the children rushed to see, and circle time developed an entirely new and especially unplanned focus. The teacher's flexibility determined her artistry.

These moments requiring creative artistry on the part of the teacher are common and are often the subject of humor and/or consternation in discussions teachers have among themselves.

Equally common, and intimately linked with the teacher-as-artist, are the times when teachers' discussions are focused on what-to-do-next questions, placing them in the role of scientists in their self-reflection and planning. Teachers draw upon their knowledge base, usually comprised of personal experience, reports of the experiences of others, and understanding of developmental theory as it is applied to practice. They draw largely upon their own work with young children for the first, discussions with colleagues for the second, and information from researchers in child development for the third. The latter is the focus for our own work, as we ask what teachers can receive from researchers that will be useful to them in planning, executing, and evaluating their teachable moments with children.

teaching as giving and receiving

All teachers want to give their students the best possible information, professional expertise, and personal attention. In turn, they hope to receive (and often do!) the pleasure of a hug, an excited "I did it!" or sparkling eyes and secret smiles as children discover ideas and master skills in the activities their teachers have planned for them.

The establishment of this ongoing giving-receiving relationship with children is one of the essential rewards of the "calling" of teaching (Noddings & Shore, 1984). John Steinbeck, in his essay in tribute to Ed Ricketts, the famed "Doc" of Cannery Row, comments about this aspect of teaching:

> It is so easy to give, so exquisitely rewarding. Receiving, on the other hand, if it be well done, requires a fine balance of self-knowledge and kindness. It requires humility and tact and great understanding of relationships. In receiving you cannot appear, even to yourself, better or stronger or wiser than the giver, although you must be wiser to do it well. . . .
>
> Ed's gift for receiving made him a great teacher. Children brought shells to him and gave him information about the shells. And they had to learn before they could tell him. In conversation you found yourself telling him things — thoughts, conjectures, hypotheses — and you found a pleased surprise at yourself for having arrived at something you were not aware you could think or know. It gave you such a good sense of participation with him that you could present him with wonder. (Steinbeck, 1941/1969, p. lxiii).

Yet teachers need to receive from sources other than the children order to fuel effectively their giving-receiving relationship with them. Teachers need to receive information from researchers that they can use in their practice of teaching. What can research tell me about this particular child (this group, this concept)? are questions often asked by teachers and just as often inadequately addressed by researchers. A preschool teacher in San Francisco comments, "Theorists and researchers in education need to cut down their resolutions to planet Earth, where teachers sometimes barely get through the day."

Too many times in our work as teachers, and in work with teachers, we have encountered the complaint that research in child development has little or no relevance to those who work with children on a daily basis. Or, even if the relevance exists, the constructs of analysis, interpretation, and writing in child development remain untranslated for the teacher.

the researcher as artist and scientist

While many emphasize the art of teaching, it is also common to focus on the science of research; yet, like teaching, research involves both qualities. The good researcher, like the good teacher, plans research carefully, conducts it artfully, and evaluates it thoroughly.

In their planning, researchers draw on their own experience and that reported by others, and on theory. Good researchers remain sensitive to subtle questions or paradoxes raised in each day's collection and analysis of data. When serendipity captures the moment and allows for creativity and spontaneity, they become excited. Finally, researchers reflect full circle on their research and on its application to the questions that generated the process to begin with. Their professional development depends on their ability to reflect on both the artistry and the scientific rigor in the work.

Good researchers in early childhood education examine concerns that are generated in practice, and they must feed the findings back into practice in order for the reflective process inherent in research to produce educational change. Individual teachers who are skillful interlocutors between children's behavior and their own practice foster the development of individuals and groups in their settings. In much the same way, researchers who are skillful interlocutors between developmental theory and teacher practice further the development of the field of early childhood education.

research as giving and receiving

There is an opportunity here for both teachers and researchers to enhance their professional development. By working in cooperation with rather than parallel to researchers, teachers can enhance their knowledge base and understanding of child development. They can offer essential feedback to researchers about the practical implications of their work, and they can help researchers to formulate questions and choose methods that are relevant to practice.

The incentive for researchers exists as well. Most researchers in child development hope to make significant contributions to the field, both theoretically and practically. Too often a researcher completes a time-consuming and/or expensive study to find that the analysis has little application in the real world. We believe that researchers want to ask relevant questions in their work and that both theory and practice can benefit from the additional reflective input that teachers have to offer. Real opportunities for reciprocal partnerships between teachers and researchers offer occasions for researchers to give relevant information and to receive critical feedback from practice.

We specify "real" opportunities for reciprocity here because we see many problems in some of the current models of "collaborative research" with teachers. From the teacher's perspective, the researcher too often maintains the power to ask the questions and interpret the data. Teachers are asked for feedback regularly about classroom processes and even research methods, but they are rarely given the opportunity to step out of their teacher role and participate fully in the reflective research role. Researchers gather information from teachers and children and then maintain both the freedom and time to transform the knowledge base and construct theory through reflection.

Although this process may be a step in the right direction, good intentions in collaborative research do not account for the polarization of roles involved in researchers being paid to think and teachers being paid to do, with little dialogue or synthesis present for either.

> "You can really have no notion how delightful it will be
> When they take us up and throw us, with the lobsters, out to sea!"
> But the snail replied, "Too far, too far!" and gave a look askance —
> Said he thanked the whiting kindly, but he would not join the dance.
> Would not, could not, would not, could not, would not join the dance.
> Would not, could not, would not, could not, could not join the dance.
>   (Carroll, *Alice in Wonderland*, 1865/1946, p. 119)

dancing on the bridge

Collaborative models are not always as limited as we have described. A few researchers have fully engaged teachers in the research process and have themselves worked with children to produce a knowledge base well grounded in each area. Examples are the work of Florio and Walsh (1981), Green and Wallat (1981), and Archer, Coffee, and Genishi (1985).

Drawing on these examples of genuine teacher-researcher roles, we invite the field of early childhood education to use the bridges that have been built between teaching and research to form firm and stable partnerships among those who have traditionally researched child development in laboratory settings and those who apply principles of theory and findings from research in their work with children.

Clarke-Stewart and Fein discuss the nature and complexity of this challenge in their chapter on "Early Childhood Programs" in the *Handbook of Child Psychology* (Mussen & Hetherington, 1983). They characterize early childhood programs as a promising basis for a "new research paradigm" in child development:

> Studies of early childhood programs require a difficult to achieve balance between theory and practice — a balance that has not yet occurred in developmental psychology. The programs offer a unique opportunity to map the theoretical domain of child development by studying systematic variation of programs and effects, in input and output, while providing the option of strengthening educational practice by extending ideas drawn from developmental theory. Focusing on the studies of these programs can help conceptualize and clarify this research paradigm in which psychologists and educators, scientists and practitioners, work reciprocally. (p. 919)

Several writers have documented strides made in the field of child development in the last three decades (Cahan, 1986; Robinson & Hom, 1979). Many of the research findings in cognitive, social, and emotional development of children have powerful implications for practice. Methodologies have become increasingly sensitive to real-world contexts and real child behavior. But, as valuable as the information reported in research journals may be, it remains incomplete unless the researcher evaluates its impact on practice and unless the teacher feeds back additional questions for the researcher to examine.

The fact remains that the paradigms for professional competence in child development research and early childhood education are very disparate. The role of teacher-researcher would allow professionals who study and teach children to partake of both reflective and active processes while advancing both theory and practice in the field (Duckworth, 1986). Much energy seems wasted now with parallel efforts to examine questions raised about the development of children.

The establishment of a productive common ground for both teaching and research in our field might well assure that the whole becomes greater than the sum of its parts. As Clarke-Stewart and Fein (1983, p. 919) express this hope, "Elegant theory may develop in tandem with sophisticated practical problem solving and general knowledge may be the end product of an ongoing exchange between general and specific knowledge, between scientist and technician."

REMAINING QUESTIONS

Our own experiences led us from the world of the teacher into that of the researcher and back again. Our role transformations led to changes in our views of teaching, the development of play, and relationships between home and school. What is needed to complement our experiences and fill out the role of teacher-researcher are reports of the experiences of researchers who have become teachers, and then returned to roles as researchers. Reflections of those who have participated in collaborative efforts of varying degrees are also valuable in formulating a realistic role for the teacher-researcher (Duckworth, 1986).

In creating this new role, one must ask the same questions regarding the relativity of art and science, giving and receiving, that we asked of each separate professional role. Different settings, situations, and questions considered might lead to differing degrees of emphasis on one role or the other.

We must ask, for example, in which cases does the teacher serve as interlocutor in translating scientific information from the researcher into artful practice? In which cases does the teacher serve the field best by asking questions for research to consider? In which cases must the researcher serve as interlocutor by translating experiences observed in classrooms into a refined and broadened knowledge base in the field of child development? In which cases can the researcher effectively draw questions from theory that can also be explored by teaching in environments for young children? Central to all of this is to ask to what degree each seeks to involve the other actively in complementary processes of teaching and research as they contribute to developing the field of early childhood education.

If we are, in fact, to choreograph a new dance between the teacher and the researcher, we must examine carefully both the music and the steps we select. Who shall lead if we should choose to dance together rather than apart? What supports must the field of early childhood education offer to teachers and researchers alike, if we are to act and reflect with sensitivity and reciprocity?

> "What matters it how far we go?" his scaly friend replied.
> "The further off from England the nearer is to France.
> There is another shore, you know, upon the other side.
> Then turn not pale, beloved snail, but come and join the dance.
> Will you, wo'n't you, will you, wo'n't you, will you join the dance?
> Will you, wo'n't you, will you, wo'n't you, will you join the dance?"
>   (Carroll, *Alice in Wonderland*, 1865/1946, p. 119)

7
the teacher
at the intersection
of change

SOME ASSUMPTIONS

In considering our new understanding of children's play and our roles
in it as teachers, we began to see that both the idea of becoming
teacher-researchers and the new knowledge to be achieved thereby
represented a departure from our normal perceptions of ourselves. In
this departure we saw a beginning — but only a beginning — of a
redefinition of the teacher's role which could have a wider application.
This redefinition entailed an examination of not only our normal
approach to our work but of some of its underlying assumptions. For
us, and we believe for the majority of early childhood teachers, these
assumptions include the following:

> The child is at the center.
> Play is seen as the child's natural curriculum.
> The child learns through active engagement with the persons and
> things of his or her world.
> Teachers, from their knowledge of the field, have the autonomy to
> adapt the curriculum to individuals and groups of learners in
> their care.
> The rationale for what is done is firmly rooted in a family of
> developmental theories derived from Erikson, Freud, Piaget,
> and Werner and also has a philosophical frame of reference
> derived from Dewey.

Our reflection on the history of early childhood education, based on these assumptions, demonstrated that it is a strong and resilient profession that has shown continuity over time and particular application. It is flexible and can accommodate to diverse learners and circumstances. Excellence *and* equity in educational options for the learner can be its natural outcome because it takes the *learner,* not *what is to be learned,* as its primary focus. We saw that the explication of these principles as a theory of practice in early childhood education had often occurred in reflection and in dialogue among teacher colleagues. We also saw a pressing need for a more adequate articulation of the theory, in order to address the problems that currently impinge on the welfare of children.

When we reviewed what had happened to early childhood education since nursery schools began to flourish, we were reminded that the assumptions we hold have been challenged from time to time. Teachers have needed to be articulate and well informed in order to refute their opponents in the past, and they must be today as well.

THE LONG DIALOGUE

Kohlberg and Mayer, in an article titled "Development as the Aim of Education" (1972), sharpened the discussion that went on as the presumed advantages of early education were being extended at that time to poor preschool children living in areas where failure in elementary school had become the norm. In two respects the state of early childhood education in the early 1970s paralleled the situation now. The play emphasis in the nursery-school curriculum was subject to criticism. The need for childcare was expanding rapidly, and the feasibility of increasing the number of childcare centers including educational components was widely discussed.

Criticism of the play emphasis had come initially and most directly from those experimental programs for poor children whose designers believed in the efficacy of the direct teaching of academic skills, using systematic schedules of reinforcement. Criticism also came from experimental programs whose orientation was less behavioristic and more developmental, often inspired by Piaget, whose designers believed that the curriculum must be organized to insure certain specific cognitive outcomes. Both of these groups maintained that, whatever intellectual or mental goals the traditional nursery schools had possessed, they had too often been overlooked in the more pervasive concerns for the child's social and emotional development.

Kohlberg and Mayer (1972) put these criticisms in new perspective by relating them to three traditions in American educational practice: the romantic or child-centered "bag-of-virtues" approach, the cultural-transmission approach, and the progressive approach. Building on the latter, they called for a recommitment to ethical and moral values in education, invoking traditional links with Dewey and the idea of education for a democratic citizenry. They endorsed Piaget and an interactionist framework as a source for practice.

curriculum models

Kohlberg and Mayer's (1972) article gave focus to the debate over the curriculum models then being tested in programs for poor children. All of the models intended to improve the eventual cognitive functioning of the children; they differed only on the means of accomplishing this.

Many preschool teachers saw an overemphasis on cognition as a threat to the "whole-child" approach and an outlook that could lead to the erosion of the traditional play curricula. On the other hand, some teachers continued to ask how one could emphasize play when the serious business of school readiness for disadvantaged children was at stake. The controversy over the models offered early childhood educators a unique opportunity to reflect on their own practice. It led to more than a decade and a half of critical examination of the child-centered curriculum.*

Meanwhile, the whole-child approach has had some important successes. One of these is Head Start, on whose advisory panels have served a number of developmentalists and psychodynamic theorists identified with early childhood education, including Barbara Biber, Bettye Caldwell, James L. Hymes, Jr., and Eveline Omwake. Another is the continuing use of curricula that, beginning as experimental programs in the sixties, have taken a strongly developmental view. Perhaps best known of these now is the High Scope Curriculum.

At the time that Kohlberg and Mayer (1972) wrote on development as the aim of education, the evaluation of the experimental programs for poor young children was a major issue. Time, the tightening of federal funds, and the insistence of early childhood developmentalists and educators (among others) that standardized tests have important

---

*See, for example, the article by Shapiro and Biber (1972), "The Education of Young Children: A Developmental-Interaction Approach," which provides a detailed and thoughtful description of the whole-child approach. Weber (1984) traces the debate and puts it in historical and societal perspective.

limitations have led to somewhat more realistic appraisals of program successes. Although Head Start has not guaranteed the children's later school success, as some of its critics thought it should, it has had a powerful influence on the parents of the children and has favorably affected the children's attitudes toward school and community.

The case for the developmentally oriented experimental programs, and for the High Scope Curriculum in particular, is a little different. When the children in these programs reached the ages of 9 to 19, the researchers from the various programs pooled their efforts to determine what had happened to the children as they were growing up. Comparison of children who had participated in the programs with other children in similar circumstances who had not revealed that those who had attended preschool were less likely to be put in special education classes, to be absent from school a lot, to drop out, or to become delinquent (Lazar & Darlington, 1982). On the basis of these studies, one can argue that experience in a high-quality, well-run preschool pays off years later, regardless of its theoretical orientation or instructional methods.

More recently, however, a small but important piece of evidence suggests that there are significant differences in the long-term consequences of certain models. Schweinhart, Weikart, and Larner (1986) compared children who had experienced the High Scope program with those in a traditional nursery school and in the Bereiter-Engelmann program. The latter emphasized direct instruction and made no special provision for play. The children in the developmentally oriented programs who were given opportunities for play were less likely to become delinquent as they grew up. It would be dangerous to generalize on the basis of a single study; but, if these results can be replicated in other studies, we will be able to say that *play* in a well-run preschool pays off in more adequate social development later on.

childcare

The success of High Scope and other developmentally based programs, together with the success of Head Start, attests to the resilience and flexibility of the developmental model in early childhood education. Such adaptability has also been demonstrated in relation to the expanding need for childcare.

Kohlberg and Mayer (1972) did not specifically address the childcare issue, but the idea that the aim of education was to promote development raised implicit questions about the function of other institutions in the child's life. One critic of the Kohlberg and Mayer position, Bereiter (1973), proposed that the proper function of education was instruction in academic skills and that the promotion of child development was best relegated to families and childcare organizations.

This position reflected, consciously or not, attitudes that had long been held by child welfare workers. From the beginning of the nursery-school movement, they had argued that the combination of childcare and nursery-school education could only result in inadequate care for the children. They based this position on their long years of experience with daycare, the roots of which go back to the 1840s, when centers or day nurseries were founded literally "to prevent young children from wandering the streets" (Scarr & Weinberg, 1986, p. 1141).

Despite opposition from child welfare, teachers with preparation in early childhood education began to assume positions in daycare as early as the 1930s. They brought to the centers informal ways of working with children that promoted the kind of learning "that occurred in a middle-class home" (Moore, 1977; Scarr & Weinberg, 1986). They also brought an emphasis on play and on an environment to facilitate it. By the 1970s child welfare and early education were linked as federal programs began to provide varying kinds of support for daycare for the disadvantaged. Federal licensing requirements, although long debated and never fully implemented, reflected the extent to which the child development, whole-child view was increasingly accepted.

At the time of the Kohlberg and Mayer (1972) article, the issues related to childcare were becoming more political. Granted that daycare ought to promote development, how could it be financed? Who would be responsible for its operation? Should center care be available to infants and toddlers as well as preschoolers? To middle-class families as well as the poor?

Over the years of the long dialogue, it appears that early childhood teachers have spoken effectively for the whole-child, developmental approach. They have demonstrated that it works. Now, continuing demands for childcare and the current crisis in public education confront us with new challenges and new opportunities.

THE CURRENT DEBATE

Many large issues impinge on children's well-being today: the widening circle of poverty, particularly of single women with children;

the general climate of terror and violence, depicted and documented in the media, surrounds the child's world — a climate that is also a reality in the daily lives of many children. The continuing menace of toxic waste and nuclear contamination persists. Changes in patterns in family life and shifts in demographic trends often pit the demands of the aged against those of children in vying for public resources to remedy the social ills experienced by both groups.

Two other major issues that threaten to affect children directly are the rapid expansion of childcare and the current crisis in public education. These issues are confounded by still others, such as the uses of technology in the classroom; the press for excellence; the continuing and expanding need for equity in educational opportunity for the handicapped, the poor, and the racially, ethnically, or linguistically different child. For example, despite widespread efforts to assure gender equity, current findings indicate that differences in boys' and girls' course choices persist in creating disparity of opportunity in math and science (Archer & Lloyd, 1985, pp. 223, 245).

Because of changing patterns in child-rearing practices in America and the concern created by the perceived decline in quality of formal education, goals and aims in education are once again up for redefinition. This redefinition occurs in the midst of profound changes in the American home.

changes in child rearing

The Children's Defense Fund (1982) reports on one aspect of change, "the four-fold increase in labor force participation of mothers with children under age six, from 12 percent in 1947 to 47% in 1980" p. 3). Projecting to the 1990s, Ruopp (1985) states that "by 1990 as many as 11 or 12 million children will need a substantial amount of care from people other than their parents" (p. 1). Commenting on current childcare scarcities, Ruopp adds that "both need and demand are outstripping supply" (p. 3). Finding caretakers for infants is particularly difficult. Family daycare, long the major resource for parents unable to arrange for care at home or with relatives, appears to be becoming scarce. Childcare centers have waiting lists steadily increasing in length.

Parents' need for childcare is joined by a growing demand for earlier educational intervention made by middle-class parents, as well as the continuing need for early intervention for the poor ("Preschool Enrollment," 1986). The increasing numbers of children in some form of care outside the home for longer periods of time continuing impact on the traditional ways we have nurtured and socialized our children, both in and out of school.

socialization in daycare

Children's social selves are constructed out of innumerable encounters with people and events of their world. Much of this socialization takes place before the age of formal schooling. Traditionally the context for this process has been informal and based largely on spontaneous play. Such play with peers and siblings was monitored more or less indirectly by parents, relatives, neighbors and teachers, who could reasonably insure children's safety at home, on neighborhood streets, and in parks and playgrounds. This primary context for socialization is rapidly changing. Far more children now spend a larger portion of their day away from home in some institutional setting. As a consequence, the character of self-directed spontaneous play with peers and siblings may be changing.

Not much is known about the character of the new social environments that are replacing the primary context of home and neighborhood. While little information is available on the character of children's play and interactions with peers and consequent socialization in childcare centers, Clarke-Stewart (1982) has reviewed the studies that have evaluated the overall effects of such programs. These studies have measured individual outcomes such as social maturity, language facility, and response to strangers. They have tended to make their assessments outside the context of the childcare setting. Other studies have assessed ecological elements of childcare environments, rating such things as the features and complexity of the physical setting and staff-child ratios (Harms & Clifford, 1980; Kritchevsky et al., 1969). Recent work that suggests the impoverishment of the daycare experience includes Suransky's ethnographic study from which she drew a composite picture of the "landscape of childcare" (1982). Schwartzman's (1978) landmark book on play includes details of an ethnographic study of a childcare center. It yielded interesting information about children's relationships to one another and to their teachers.

The early childhood educator knows that "play helps children make their lives meaningful." The observation and study of play can help "adults understand the meanings children give to their experiences and can give guidance to adults" (Sponseller, 1982, p. 231). The possible consequences of programs that fail to provide child-initiated learning activities and play suggest that expanding childcare settings be monitored closely.

Many programs bring with them points of view, sets of goals, and ways of evaluation that are in many ways antithetical to good practice in early education and care, for example, requiring 3-year-olds to sit for long periods of time in large group meetings. Unlike the traditional preschool, they often have little investment in play as an instrument of development. The current encounter between differing orientations in education point to the need for articulation of criteria with respect to play that are based on sound theory.

The following anecdote from a somewhat older daycare child reflects current concerns about what may be happening to play in many daycare programs:

ADULT.   I hear you're going to the Marina today.
CHILD.   . . . and we're going ice skating, too.
ADULT.   Oh, that's great!
CHILD.   . . . and tomorrow we're going to *Cinderella.*
ADULT.   Oh, really?
CHILD.   . . . and then we get a day off.

We suspect the overprogramming implied here is typical of daycare experience for many children of all ages. If so, what happens to spontaneous play with peers and siblings, long believed by developmentalists to be a major vehicle for socialization? Too much intervention may be a corollary to safe supervision in group settings. If so, what happens to children's self-direction in learning, and what happens to the privacy necessary for solitary play?

One of the questions that arises with the widening need for childcare is, Who will fill the need? In many cases the public schools will enter the field. With an already established track record in schooling, suitable sites, and administrative organization, there is much to recommend them. The research by Schweinhart et al. (1986), however, suggests the adverse effects of premature introduction of direct instruction techniques. We wonder if public schools have the means by which to modify their methods. Other arrangements are emerging, for example, some combination of agencies such as schools and youth organizations or private vendors utilizing public spaces for childcare. The number of corporations involved in childcare increases steadily. A diversity of kinds of care may be desirable in order to serve the needs of diverse families, but questions remain as to who will monitor these settings and how.

the crisis in public education

Despite the fact that some public schools are already expanding to provide childcare for school-age children and that some are operating such programs for younger children, childcare as a function of public education arouses considerable skepticism. Critics fear that direct instruction and elementary-school organization will dominate the program, curtailing the children's opportunities for play. As they see it, some of the recently established educational programs for 4-year-olds in large cities confirm their fears (Fiske, 1986).

Critics are not only concerned about an overemphasis on direct instruction but also about the ineffectiveness that pervades so much of public education. Why attach new responsibilities to an institution that seems to have been in crisis at least since the Sputnik scare of the 1950s?

Thoughtful early childhood teachers will be wary of overgeneralizing from screaming headlines about the current crisis. Many schools, and certainly many teachers, continue to be effective; but they do so against great odds. As the president of the National Education Association, which represents 1.8 million teachers, writes,

> Our schools today are structurally decrepit, still shaped by an organizational model appropriate to 19th century industry. That model does little to enliven the imagination. It does much to stifle innovation. It does little to encourage collegial cooperation. It does much to intensify isolation. (Futrell, 1986, p. 6)

As early childhood teachers reflect on the public education crisis, they can see certain discrepancies to their own situation and also certain parallels. Some early childhood teachers are caught in the outdated structures Futrell describes, but many are in situations where they have considerable autonomy to make educational decisions. For example, it is up to them to decide the proper balance between spontaneous play and other activities in their curriculum.

Not all early childhood teachers aspire to teach in public school. (Monighan-Nourot, the reader will recall, chose to leave her position there.) But most early childhood teachers would like to have the employment status and the benefits that accrue to public-school teachers. As they move toward more professional standing, they may find lessons for themselves in some of the reforms proposed for resolving the current crisis in public education.

Futrell (1986) notes that most of the reform efforts so far have resulted in more regulations from state offices; less authority for teachers, parents, and local agencies; and more emphasis on what can be counted or measured easily. The report of the Carnegie Commission (Tucker & Mandel, 1986) provides an exception to this general trend since it emphasizes the full participation of the teacher in decision making.

In commenting on reforms that would enlarge teachers' responsibilities, Giroux and McLaren (1986) note an ominous silence regarding the role of the teacher as intellectual. Also regrettable is the failure to link reforms to a "legacy bequeathed us by educational forebears, such as John Dewey and George Counts" (p. 215). Equally regrettable is the fact that some teachers do not see themselves as "intellectual workers," choosing instead to participate in the abdication of responsibility inherent in student tracking and teacherproof educational technologies. As we see it, both the advancement of the early childhood teacher as a professional and the protection of play in the early childhood curriculum call for teachers who are intellectually active. They will draw on developmental and other research related to young children. As individuals and in collaboration with colleagues in their own and other centers of learning, they will participate in the research that is so vital to good education and care for young children.

research on play crucial

In asserting the importance of research on play, we have in mind both the kind that yields normative generalizations about the nature of children's development and the kind that is specific to particular groups of children in particular settings.

The first kind of research continues a tradition that began when psychologists conducted systematic observations of children in nursery schools, in order to study their manifestations of fear, sympathy, aggression, and friendship. More recently researchers have drawn on their knowledge of children's play to investigate such questions as how children's moral and social understanding develops (Damon, 1977; Denzin, 1977; Nucci & Turiel, 1978) and how children are able to adopt the points of view of others (Gelman, 1983). Knowledge of developmental research across cognitive, affective, and social domains is essential if early childhood educators are to be effective in asserting that development as well as education should be the aim of childcare. This is a wonderful way to heighten the current debate!

Also important to the early childhood educator, as advocate to policy makers, is knowledge of recent advances in theory and method that have come from linguists and psycholinguists and from ethno-graphic and pragmatic studies of human communication. Re-searchers in this area are reexamining the vitality of traditional observational, psychometric, ethological, and clinical methods and are proposing new applications of these methods that are contrib-uting to our understanding of the complexity of human interaction.

Because of the great diversity in settings for early childhood education and care, we think that research that is specific to particular settings has great value. For example, Suransky's (1982) study of five different childcare centers revealed considerable evidence of what she termed "the erosion of childhood." Knowledge of the good effects of existing programs on the children's play enables those responsible for a center to defend it against unsuitable innovations. Such knowledge can also serve as a point of departure for needed modification in programs where the effects are not good.

It also should be borne in mind that, although observational study in a single center is not likely to yield data that will be directly useful to policy makers, generalizations based on the accumulation of information from a number of centers could become a powerful influence on policy makers.

Close examination of the play in a particular setting also provides information on the ways the children are receiving the information and values of the culture. Developmental theorists know that one cannot "teach" culture to young children, although they are very effective "learners" of it. To influence the transmission of culture to the young, one needs to have ways of discovering what it is children know and can understand. Play provides a window on the ways that children mediate social knowledge. It is a primary means for the child to integrate and accommodate new information.

In early childhood education, where the child's developmental needs are the central locus of an emergent curriculum, the educator has some intrinsic safeguards against error that may not be available in later years of schooling where the generation of curriculum becomes increasingly external to the student. Such safeguards work most effectively when the teacher monitors the play for evidence of the adequacy of the match between the child's development and the curriculum.

NEW RESOURCES

We have by no means exhausted the kinds of research, both large and small scale, that need to be done to support the place of play in early childhood education and care. Rather, we have implied, as in previous chapters, the importance of the teacher as collaborator or as teacher-researcher. The teacher may well ask, "What are the resources for all this? Where can I find help?"

collaborative research

As we have noted here and in other chapters, we regard the growing abundance of child development research related to the age period from birth to 8 years, and particularly that dealing with play, as an important resource for the teacher. We have also commented that new research methods, particularly ethnography, seem well adapted to classroom use. Some research using these new methods has involved teachers in a more collaborative relationship with the researcher (Gilmore & Glatthorn, 1982). The beginning notion of reciprocity between the researcher and all those whom she studies has led Lather (1986) to suggest boldly that in research there can be "no intimacy without reciprocity" (p. 263).

If a teacher finds the notion of collaborative research enticing, the next question is how and where to find a collaborator. As the saying goes, "it takes two to tango." Obviously some teachers, particularly those in some childcare situations, find it difficult and sometimes impossible to make even brief notes on what goes on in the children's play. Or could some rescheduling, some recruitment of volunteers (grandparents? students from upper grades? parents whose employment allows them some free time? students from child development courses?) enable two teachers to collaborate as Monighan-Nourot and her colleague did? Is the clustering of teachers in conversation that one sometimes sees on busy playgrounds essential to their sharing of center concerns, or could one or more take responsibility for systematic observation?

When it comes to locating a collaborator who is already a researcher, the teacher will likely find it necessary to take the lead and perhaps some rebuffs as well. Researchers and would-be researchers at community colleges, colleges, and universities often complain about the difficulty of finding subjects for their studies. They are not accustomed to being approached by teachers with researchable questions and available classrooms full of subjects. Some researchers, teachers will find, are too engrossed in their own questions or too inflexible to enter a truly reciprocal relationship. But now and then one or two will snap at the opportunity. No harm in asking and, incidentally, in changing their stereotypes of classroom teachers.

professional organizations and publications

Another resource for the early childhood teacher is the professional organization to which he belongs, such as the Association for Childhood Education International (ACEI), with its roots going back to the beginning of kindergartens in the last half of the 19th century; the Southern Association for Children under Six (SACUS); the National Association for the Education of Young Children (NAEYC). All these organizations have local groups that meet regularly, a program of publications, and annual conferences. All are committed to the protection of children's rights to play.

NAEYC, for example, had its origins in a small committee of nursery-school educators (mostly university based) who met together in the mid-1920s to establish standards for nursery-school education. Over the years it has grown to a membership of over 50,000. Evidence for what we see as a continuing dialogue among practitioners is nowhere more evident than in the well-attended conferences of the NAEYC, where lively if not heated exchanges around issues of practice, policy, and advocacy frequently occur. Its diverse membership, encompassing a broad range of professionals and nonprofessionals, including parents, can be seen as both one of its strengths as well as a possible weakness. In any event, because of or in spite of this broad spectrum of membership, NAEYC has managed to keep its feet well on the ground while still being able to make complex theoretical issues accessible to all its membership. It can give voice to the early educator and caregiver's understanding of the proper "aims of education" with respect to young children.

Through the resources of the NAEYC, the early childhood educator can take an advocacy position in the vanguard in establishing criteria for good professional practice in expanding daycare and early education programs, even as the push for formal schooling moves into the preschool. The recently developed accreditation criteria provide much-needed minimal standards, subject to improvement and refinement as their acceptance grows. The process of self-evaluation associated with them increases the possibilities for continuing growth in quality.

In addition, there are professional journals such as *Young Children, Childhood Education,* and *The Early Childhood Research Quarterly* that offer educators access to information about advances in both the practical and theoretical domains. These journals serve as a forum for dialogue on issues of professional importance as well.

TOWARD A THEORY OF PRACTICE

The NAEYC's recent establishment of *The Early Childhood Research Quarterly* attests to increasing recognition of the important role of research in the professionalization of the early childhood teacher and in movement toward a theory of practice.

When teachers make their own systematic observations and ask their own questions, they begin to be architects of their own practice, finding ways to link what occurs in their classroom to theoretical propositions about development as they analyze and interpret what they have observed. In sharing and reflecting on their observations with other colleagues, teachers participate in a critical dialogue wherein they can begin to find the means to weigh the importance of what they observe. *The Early Childhood Research Quarterly* was begun expressly to offer teachers such a forum.

Many early educators over the years have had the autonomy and opportunity to engage in their work in this way. If early education is to feature development as its aim, the teacher needs such freedom. Duckworth (1986) emphasizes this point as she dreams about the high-school teacher, thinking of the interaction she would like to see between the teacher and the learner. She defines the work of the teacher in much the same way as one might define a researcher who takes the study of human learning as her subject.

> This kind of researcher would be a teacher in the sense of caring about some part of the world and how it works enough to want to make it accessible to others; she would be fascinated by the questions of how to engage people in it and how people make sense of it; she would have time and resources to pursue these questions to the depth of her interest, to write what she learned, and to contribute to theoretical and pedagogical discussions on the nature and development of human learning. (p. 494)

Duckworth knows that, as things are presently constituted in most schools, with the possible exception of early childhood education, "It is a rare school teacher who has either the freedom or the time to think of her teaching as research, since much of her autonomy has been withdrawn in favor of the policies set by anonymous standard setters and test givers" (1986, pp. 293–294). For many it is easier to choose to let others take responsibility through ability grouping and prepackaged curricula.

Early childhood teachers, we believe, still have the opportunity, if they choose, to build upon the long tradition in which observations, reflections, anecdotes, and writings constituted the available theory of practice. Griffin (1982) and Paley (1984) have so chosen. Others will continue, drawing on the wider resources now available and making the theory more explicit and more reflective of current complex realities.

CONFRONTING CHANGES
IN THEORY AND PRACTICE

The early childhood teacher once again confronts the intersection of change, in both theory and practice. Play seems a natural beginning point, since it is central both to current developmental research and to dialogues about practice.

Early childhood educators have long benefitted from their close ties to developmental and psychodynamic theory. This is nowhere more evident than in the richness of appropriate curriculum activities and materials — available to invite the child's exploration within the motivating context of play — that one witnesses in young children's programs worldwide. These curricula have been extrapolated from the theoretical constructs that early childhood educators inherited. They emerge in developmental programs that are rich and varied, resilient enough to adapt to a broad range of learners, and flexible enough to respect and accommodate the early nurturing practices of diverse cultures and peoples.

In the United States, the theory that supports this practice now needs to be articulated more fully so that points of conflict and convergence with the tenets of later, more formal schooling methods may be resolved and synthesized. Without an overt theory of practice, justification for what teachers do is based on confused and naive notions that groundlessly invoke "art," "craft," or "science." The current expansion of childcare and the extension of elementary and formal schooling into the preschool endanger play in developmentally based programs that lack a clear rationale for what is done.

Although the quality of play cannot be measured by pupil outcomes on standardized tests, accountability demands adequate means of evaluation. Typical assessment instruments are too gross to measure play, which may be as ephemeral as "angel's hair." But it is just possible that as our research advances we will discover that play has a strength and resilience that reveals itself to the touch of those who respect its aims.

By seizing the opportunity to become better and better informed about play, early childhood teachers have much to gain for children. Only a firm foundation in research and theory guarantees the diversity in program structure that enhances the development of young children.

By seizing the opportunity to become teacher-researchers, early childhood teachers also have much to gain for themselves. Play is an important building block in the theory of early childhood education practice. Can we not see the teacher-researcher as an architect in building that theory? And is not that an important professional advance?

8
conclusion

We have been discussing young children's play as central to their development and, consequently, central to their education. This view of play is consistent with views expressed over the past 60 years by developmental theorists such as Piaget and Erikson, and educators such as Isaacs, Biber, and Weikart. It is antithetical to the more widely held idea of play as "time out from the work of education," recess for both students and teachers. When play is considered "time out," it is easy to see why so many administrators, teachers of older students, and parents devalue it when they walk into the kindergarten classroom to find the teacher and a group of students happily munching on imaginary pieces of birthday cake at a pretend party. They often ask, Is this why we send kids to school? Is this why we pay teachers?

How do we say yes? Programs that put a heavy emphasis on play *do* place a heavy burden on the teacher. It is crucial that we as teachers become able to articulate reasons for this emphasis on play, which at present is primarily based on our understanding of developmental theory. As Fein and Schwartz (1982) suggest, we should lead from developmental theory to a theory of practice, from general principles to specific activities for specific children, to our plans for Monday.

As we become better informed we are better able to turn from platitudes such as "play meets the needs of the whole child" or "play is the child's work" to clearly stated explanations of how Marie's use of a pretend napkin to wipe the pretend birthday cake crumbs off her pants indicates a growing ability to use abstract symbols, "and yes, that's similar to the ability she will need in reading and math." Not only can we articulate these reasons to others, we can also "plan for Monday." For example, we want to observe Marie in order to assess whether she is now using fewer representational objects in her pretend play than she was last fall. We may also check our notes to see whether she has spent time in the block area recently.

Initially, when we turned to the literature to answer questions we and other teachers frequently ask about play, it appeared that we were examining a narrow though interesting field. We asked, How can I tell if it's play? and found discussions of features such as active engagement, intrinsic motivation, and attention to means, not ends. We asked, How does play develop? and found that, as children develop, their play involves the use of more abstract symbols and demonstrates an increased ability to maintain a shared perspective with playmates. We asked, How can I explain play? and read the work of theorists who view play as a chance for children to develop mastery, to incorporate and consolidate experiences.

Upon further reflection, we find that the answers to our questions about play relate inseparably to our view of development and to our philosophy regarding the goals of education. These answers contribute toward a theory of practice.

It is not accidental that educators such as Isaacs promoted activity characterized by intrinsic motivation, nonliteral behavior, and active engagement. Certainly there is great agreement among early childhood educators that the educational process should support children's motivation, creativity, and ability to use symbols. Similarly, research indicates that children's play demonstrates their social, cognitive, and physical development and suggests that it fosters development as well. The description of how play develops is a mirror of the way development occurs. For example, the 3-year-old girls in Scales's "Basic Cooking" indicate their wish to play, negotiate an understanding of what they will play, and then enact it. The length and complexity of this interaction is far greater than that of typical 2-year-olds.

Based upon the parallels between our discussion of the development of play as a specific topic and the description of children's development in the broadest sense, we can begin to develop a more complete rationale for the central role of play in programs for young children.

Our own efforts as teacher-researchers are attempts to further a theory of practice. The descriptions of our research were not included here as models of exemplary research. Instead, we have shared them as examples of attempts to answer questions that arose in our programs — questions for which developmental theory did not provide specific answers. To answer our questions we had to become much more knowledgeable about theory, previous research, and research methodology. As teacher-researchers we were in an optimal position to go from more abstract and general ideas about how development takes place to more concrete and specific educational practices.

Research led us to reconsider the way we looked at the issues we were studying and to expand our vision to include new questions. Although we had not purposely planned complementary research, we continually found that each of us drew upon the insights of the others.

As we became more knowledgeable about theory, we began to see the interrelationships of our own limited contributions. For example, Scales and Monighan-Nourot both examined the ways in which children begin to take the perspective of another and thereby become more skillful in playing with others.

All of our work also related to issues of practice that we face daily. We had always known that "free play for children" was not "free time for teachers." We found myriad ways of improving our planning for children's play, reconsidering how we arranged the environment and how we intervened. In addition to implications for issues relating specifically to play, we examined implications for school practices such as assessment of children's development and linkages between school and home.

In this process, parallels between research and teaching became more apparent. We discussed the nature of research and teaching as both artistic and scientific endeavors. In so doing we recognized that good practice always involves research; good research on practice always involves teachers and teaching. Our tentative conversations about "bridging the worlds of teacher and researcher" grew bolder as we saw more possibilities not only for teacher-researchers like ourselves, but also for true collaborative, reciprocal efforts between teacher-researchers and researchers, creative "dancing on the bridge."

Last, as discussed in Chapter 7, we looked at play research in the larger context of the lives of children. Again, rather than an interesting side road, we came to view our role as teachers as being played at the intersection of change and we came to see the place of play as central to educational practice.

Major issues affecting the lives of young children today include the expansion of daycare and the crisis in public education. With each comes a push for curtailing or changing children's opportunities for play. Although early childhood educators have always intuitively recognized the importance of play, our failure to validate its importance systematically has led to the frustrating need to defend it each time educational changes occur.

As teachers, we have researched some ways in which children learn from their playful, active involvement with people and things. We have observed the central role of play in children's development and are familiar with research on outcomes of programs that promote play. We have had much to say about policy issues and have felt knowledgeable and articulate in promoting the place of play in early childhood education and care. Our own experiences have led us to reexamine the concept of professionalism. As teacher-researchers we have begun to take ourselves more seriously, and so have others.

Practitioners are the best sources of concrete examples generated from developmental abstractions (Fein & Schwartz, 1982), and our research necessitated that we continually improve our ability to do this. As we did so, we became better translators of developmental theory. Good programs for young children are the "enactment of specific developmental principles" (Biber, 1979, p. 156, emphasis added). We began to see ourselves as "enactors" with knowledge of theory and practice, competent to act at policy-making levels, at the intersection of educational change.

Much of this professional growth came with the reflection that it is part of the research process we have described. For each of us, group discussions were high points. We continued to get together, even after we finished the research. This book evolved from these continuing conversations. Each chapter, except for the case studies, is based on tape-recorded conversations. We conclude this last chapter with highlights from our latest discussion. We invite you to continue it.

VAN HOORN. Suppose we knew about more play, how would things be different?

ALMY. I think that we'd see environments that would not be so stereotyped. Paying close attention to children's play leads to a more individualized program.

SCALES. I think we're going to see the housekeeping corner for a long time because it's based on the young child's home experiences and serves as an important transition to school, but it certainly could undergo some transitions that reflect differing cultural traditions and our better understanding of play.

ALMY. Also, if we knew more about play, you wouldn't see as much play going on without anybody's being aware of it.

SCALES. You know, in my study I expected to make a lot of changes, make things better. Instead I gradually came to discover a beautiful logic to it. We wound up retaining the essential features in our new play yard. But we became *much* more conscious of *why* we did what we did. This conceptual grasp of our work made us more creative in a coherent way and helped us steer away from variations derived from mere novelty, like adding red coloring to water. By thinking of our work as research we, like Vygotsky's child at play, had risen above our ordinary level.

ALMY. That's so, Barbara. You know, I remember visiting your center over 40 years ago, soon after Catherine Landreth designed it. And today, it looks a lot the same. That sure demonstrates the wisdom in the early childhood education tradition.

VAN HOORN. As I learned more about what Barbara was doing, I saw how powerful even a seemingly slight intervention could be. That really affected me. But is it conceivable that we could find out more than we need to know? Will we be invading children's privacy?

MONIGHAN-NOUROT. I would guess that we as teachers often go through predictable stages. You know how it is when you first discover something — you see everything in those terms . . .

ALMY. I remember, many years ago, discovering Freud and, for a while, looking at play only from a psychodynamic point of view . . .

MONIGHAN-NOUROT. Yes, that's what I mean. At that point you intervene too much. But then you go on to a more mature stage in your understanding. Your intervention becomes more thoughtful, more sensitive.

ALMY. For example, if we knew more, we might decide that at some point you could do more with a certain theme or story.

MONIGHAN-NOUROT. Different themes seem to draw more at different ages. For instance, I've always wondered why 3-year-olds find *The Three Bears* so appealing.

SCALES. I was thrilled with what Paley did with this thematic thing — you know — generating the drama themes for circle from the kids' own dramatic play! She uses drama drawn from traditional stories such as *The Three Bears*. I think the use of drama in the preschool is going to open up marvelous possibilities. Drama will be a lot more than doing "plays" and "skits," where the emphasis is on performance. This new drama is going to draw on the native logic of play and will help us understand ourselves and discover what children know and understand, what children need and what they can do! And it's going to be as beautiful and authentic as children's art.

MONIGHAN-NOUROT.   This has tremendous implications for choosing books, for teaching children to read. We need to look at how play hooks in with the other areas of the curriculum like reading and math, how play as well as exploration can help children develop concepts. Teachers would then be in a much stronger position to develop their curriculum based on what children do spontaneously in their play.

VAN HOORN.   Preschool teachers who have had more experience doing this could act as resource people to K–2 teachers. They could help other teachers appreciate the play that happens in the classroom and particularly on the playground. That's about the only time some older children get to participate in dramatic and constructive play . . .

MONIGHAN-NOUROT.   And yet, when older children come into kindergarten classes as cross-age tutors, often the first things they go to are the blocks and the housekeeping corner. What does that tell us about play for school-age children?

SCALES.   I have a wonderful anecdote about older kids and the dress-up corner. Back in the 1970s I worked as an arts consultant to a supposedly innovative alternative school where many of the children came from single-parent families where the household was headed by a woman. An extraordinary thing happened when I set up a housekeeping corner. Many of the 11-year-old boys began dressing up regularly in female attire, which created a great deal of pandemonium and friction between the older and younger children. This innovative school's solution to this problem was to remove the dress-up clothes! In the future I think we're going to be able to use information like this more effectively to develop play curricula that would better serve kids' efforts to integrate ambiguities in their social knowledge.

MONIGHAN-NOUROT.   If we look more carefully at play, we'll be less likely to say "Let's get rid of it" when we see examples that make us uncomfortable. If we become more systematic in our observations, take more of a research view . . .

VAN HOORN.   We've gone right back to the point of the importance of the teacher in research — either as teacher-researcher or else collaborating with researchers.

ALMY.   We don't think that everyone in early childhood education would be a teacher-researcher. I would hope that everyone in the program would know what was going on and share.

MONIGHAN-NOUROT.   Sure . . . observing and contributing anecdotes . . .

VAN HOORN.   Being involved would help renew teachers, prevent burnout. Teachers would find that they were learning more about the kids and more about themselves.

MONIGHAN-NOUROT.   In chatting with friends with whom I taught 15 years ago, I'm amazed at our accumulated knowledge. We really have a lot to contribute to the field.

VAN HOORN.   When teachers recognize that they have a lot to give to collaborative efforts, it becomes a self-actualizing process. They develop even more to give.

MONIGHAN-NOUROT.   That's why teachers enjoy being master teachers. It's a lot of work, but it's a chance to reflect on how much you know and to do something with it.

ALMY.   Yes. In discussions of teacher authority, a major point has always been the importance of this knowledge base.

SCALES.   In the preschool of the future I think the teacher will more readily accept the role of intellectual worker. As the teacher begins thinking of herself in this more autonomous way, she will move in and out of the contexts of the researcher's role, being aware that she is a researcher of human learning who is making various research and observation paradigms her own. Seeing her role as one that no one else can perform, she will find the ways to reflect on and examine her work and how it influences children. She will work through her professional associations with her colleagues, in order to find a way to open time to pursue her work, such as by taking sabbaticals and leaves for study.

MONIGHAN-NOUROT.   Remember the discussion we had a couple of months ago about setting up an institute where early childhood educators could come for a summer or a semester to work with other teachers and researchers? You might have a lab school. Then teachers could take those techniques back to their own settings.

VAN HOORN.   Research would also be a chance to collect information that was personally interesting to individual teachers, such as, What happened to the kids who went through my program?

ALMY.   Research is a very active way for teachers to respond to emerging issues. . . . So many children today are single children coming from homes where there is little opportunity for traditional neighborhood play . . .

MONIGHAN-NOUROT.   . . . and going to daycare centers where they are segregated by age. I've discussed this a lot with a friend of mine who directs a large after-school daycare program. We dream about trying "family clusters," with a home set up in a special area of the room. What kind of dramatic play would you get? Would you have a 5-year-old playing in an idiosyncratic way while the 11-year-old designed a special costume for himself and planned out the performance?

VAN HOORN.   Or what about "no-play" programs? What's the effect on the child's behavior at school if the child doesn't get opportunities for self-structured play after school? On the other hand, what about programs that promote play to the exclusion of other areas?

ALMY. If we work hard to integrate play consciously, we could overdo play. Remember Sutton-Smith talking about making cognitive labor out of play? Maybe this applies to making it social labor, too.

VAN HOORN. Play could become too serious a business? "At this school we take play very seriously."

ALMY. There are many things that we expect children to learn, quite apart from their play. Perhaps we will become more skillful in deciding what things should be taught through discussion, exploration, rote learning, and example, as well as through play.

MONIGHAN-NOUROT. Paley was concerned about how to balance play in the curriculum with other things like puzzles and art projects.

SCALES. Like Paley, we have extended the play period for an extra 15 minutes this year and are finding now that children seem much more willing and excited about our teacher-directed activities like stories and games. We haven't had a 4-year-old uprising against story time for a couple of years. They are also settling into a very structured music class much more readily.

ALMY. I've been thinking as we're talking that in this book maybe we've oversimplified. Changing established roles isn't easy. Maybe you need to be thinking of another book based on the experiences that teachers have when they try to change existing structures . . .

MONIGHAN-NOUROT. . . . based on teachers' experiences of doing research in their own classrooms. In this landscape of the future, teachers would feel that research is serving their needs because it feeds back into their classrooms. They would feel that the scarce resources that are available for research were benefitting children

VAN HOORN. Yes. Our basic concern is what is right for kids — how we can be better advocates for kids so that changes result in better programs. I think that's why we've all found the areas of "play" and "teacher-researcher" so engrossing. The more you know about play, the more you know that you are doing the right thing.

MONIGHAN-NOUROT. You're not playing with the kids just to play — in the sense of abdicating your responsibility. You are being responsible.

references

Alexander, D. (1985, November). *Children's computer drawings — Are they art?* Paper presented at the annual conference of the National Association for the Education of Young Children, New Orleans, LA.

Ames, L., & Learned, J. (1946). Imaginary companions and related phenomena. *Journal of Genetic Psychology, 69,* 147–167.

Archer, C., Coffee, S., & Genishi, C. (1985). Research currents: Responding to children. *Language Arts, 62*(3), 270–276.

Archer, J., & Lloyd, B. (1985). *Sex and gender.* Cambridge, England: Cambridge University Press.

Avedon, E. M., & Sutton-Smith, B. (1971). *The study of games.* New York: John Wiley.

Bakeman, R., & Brownlee, J. R. (1980). The strategic use of parallel play: A sequential analysis. *Child Development, 51,* 873–878.

Barnes, K. E. (1971). Preschool play norms: A replication. *Developmental Psychology, 5,* 99–103.

Bateson, G. A. (1976). A theory of play and fantasy. In J. S. Bruner, A. Jolly, & K. Sylva (Eds.), *Play: Its role in development and evolution* (pp. 119–129). New York: Basic Books.

Beckwith, L. (1985). Parent-child interaction and social-emotional development. In C. C. Brown & A. W. Gottfried (Eds.), *Play interactions: The role of toys and parent involvement in children's development* (Pediatric Roundtable, 11) (pp. 152–159). Skillman, NJ: Johnson and Johnson Baby Products.

Bereiter, C. (1973, December). Must we educate? *Phi Delta Kappan, 55,* 233–236.

Biber, B. (1979). The preschool-education component of Head Start: Introduction. In E. Zigler & J. Valentine (Eds.), *Project Head Start: A legacy of the War on Poverty* (pp. 155–161). New York: The Free Press.

Biber, B., & Franklin, M. (1967). The relevance of developmental and psychodynamic concepts to the education of the preschool child. *Journal of the American Academy of Child Psychiatry, 6,* 5–24.

Blum, M. S. (1983). *The day care dilemma.* Lexington, MA: Lexington Books.

Brazelton, T. B. (1974). *Toddlers and parents.* New York: Dell Publishing Co.

Brazelton, T. B. (1982). Joint regulation of neonate-parent behavior. In E. Z. Tronick (Ed.), *Social interchange in infancy. Affect, cognition, and communication* (pp. 7–23). Baltimore, MD: University Park Press.

Brenner, J., & Mueller, E. (1982). Shared meaning in boy toddler's peer relations. *Child Development, 53*(2), 380–391.

Bretherton, I. (Ed.) (1984). *Symbolic play: The development of social understanding.* Orlando, FL: Academic Press.

Bruner, J. S. (1972). The nature and uses of immaturity. *American Psychologist, 27,* 687–708.

Bruner, J. S. (1976). Peekaboo and the learning of rule structures. In J. S. Bruner, A. Jolly, & K. Sylva (Eds.), *Play: Its role in development and evolution* (pp. 277–285). New York: Basic Books.

Burridge, K. O. L. (1976). A Tangu game. In J. S. Bruner, A. Jolly, & K. Sylva (Eds.), *Play: Its role in development and evolution* (pp. 364–366). New York: Basic Books

Call, J., & Marschak, M. (1966). Styles and games in infancy. *Journal of the American Academy of Child Psychiatry,* 193–210.

Carroll, L. (1946). *Alice in wonderland.* New York: Random House. (Originally published 1865)

Children's Defense Fund. (1982). *Employed parents and their children: A data book.* Washington, DC: Children's Defense Fund.

Cicourel, A. (1974). *Language use and school performance.* New York: Academic Press.

Clarke-Stewart, A. (1982). *Daycare.* Cambridge, MA: Harvard University Press.

Clarke-Stewart, A., & Fein, G. (1983). Early childhood programs. In P. H. Mussen & E. M. Heatherington (Eds.), *Handbook of child psychology* (Vol. 4). New York: John Wiley.

Clarke-Stewart, A., & Hevey, C. M. (1981). Longitudinal relations in repeated observations of mother-child interactions from 1 to $2^{1}/2$ years. *Developmental Psychology, 17,* 127–145.

Clements, D. (1986). *The computer in early and primary education.* Englewood Cliffs, NJ: Prentice-Hall.

Connolly, J., & Doyle, A. (1984). Relation of social fantasy play to social competence in preschoolers. *Developmental Psychology, 20*(5), 797–806.

Cook-Gumperz, J. (1978). *Tea partying: Recognition of naturally ordered activities.* Unpublished manuscript. University of California, Berkeley.

Cook-Gumperz, J., & Corsaro, W. (1976). Social-ecological constraints on children's communication strategies. In *Papers on language and context* (Working Paper #46). Berkeley: Language Behavior Research Laboratory, University of California.

Cook-Gumperz, J., & Gumperz, J. (1982). Introduction: Language and the communication of social identity. In J. Gumperz (Ed.), *Language and social identity* (Vol. 2) (pp. 1–21). Cambridge: Cambridge University Press.

Cordero, F. V., & Panopia, I. (1976). *General sociology: Focus on the Philippines.* Quison City, The Philippines: KEN, Inc.

Corsaro, W. (1979). We're friends, right? Children's use of access rituals in a nursery school. *Language in Society, 8,* 315–336.

Corsaro, W. A. (1985). *Friendship and peer culture in the early years.* Norwood, NJ: Ablex.

Curry, N. E. (1986). Where have all the players gone? In N. E. Curry (Ed.), *The feeling child: Affective development* (pp. 93–111). New York: Haworth Press.

Curry, N. E., & Arnaud, S. (1984). Play in developmental preschool settings. In T. Yawkey & A. Pelligrini (Eds.), *Child's play: Developmental and applied* (pp. 273–291). Hillside, NJ: Lawrence Erlbaum.

Damon, W. (1977). *The social world of the child.* San Francisco: Jossey-Bass.

Dansky, J. L., & Silverman, W. I. (1975). The effects of play on associative fluency in preschool-aged children. *Developmental Psychology, 11,* 104.

Denzin, N. K. (1977). *Childhood socialization.* San Francisco: Jossey-Bass.

DiPietro, J. (1981). Rough and tumble play: A function of gender. *Developmental Psychology, 17,* 50–58.

Duckworth, E. (1986, November). Teaching as research. *Harvard Educational Review, 56,* 481–495.

Dunn, J. (1985). Pretend play in the family. In C. Brown & A. Gottfried (Eds.), *Play interactions: The role of toys and parental involvement in children's development* (Pediatric Roundtable, 11) (pp. 79–87). Skillman, NJ: Johnson and Johnson Baby Products.

Dunn, J., & Dale, N. (1984). "I a daddy": 2-year-old's collaboration in joint pretend with sibling and with mother. In I. Bretherton (Ed.), *Symbolic play: The development of social understanding* (pp. 131–158). New York: Academic Press.

Eifermann, R. R. (1970). Cooperativeness and egalitarianism in kibbutz children's games. *Human Relations, 23,* 579–587.

Elder, J. L., & Pederson, D. R. (1978). Preschool children's use of objects in symbolic play. *Child Development, 49,* 500–504.

Elkind, D. (1981). *The hurried child.* Reading, MA: Addison-Wesley.

Ericksen, F. (1977, May). Some approaches to inquiry in school-community ethnography. *Anthropology and Education Quarterly, 3*(2), 58–69.

Erikson, E. H. (1950). *Childhood and society.* New York: W. W. Norton.

Ervin-Tripp, S. (1983). *Activity structure as scaffolding for children's second language learning.* Unpublished manuscript, University of California, Berkeley.

Fein, G. (1975). A transformational analysis of pretending. *Developmental Psychology, 11,* 291–296.

Fein, G. (1979). Play and the acquisition of symbols. In L. Katz, M. Glockner, C. Watkins, & M. Spencer (Eds.), *Current topics in early childhood education* (Vol. 2) (pp. 195–226). Norwood, NJ: Ablex. (ERIC Document Reproduction Service No. ED 152 431.)

Fein, G. (1981). Pretend play in childhood: An integrative review. *Child Development, 52,* 1095–1118.

Fein, G. (1984). The self-building potential of pretend play or "I got a fish, all by myself." In T. Yawkey & A. Pellegrini (Eds.), *Child's play: Developmental and applied* (pp. 125–142). Hillsdale, NJ: Lawrence Erlbaum.

Fein, G. (1985a). The affective psychology of play. In C. C. Brown & A. W. Gottfried (Eds.), *Play interactions: The role of toys and parent involvement in children's development* (Pediatric Roundtable, 11) (pp. 19–30). Skillman, NJ: Johnson and Johnson Baby Products.

Fein, G. (1985b, April). *Logo instructing; a constructivist view.* Paper presented at the Annual Meeting of the American Educational Research Association, Chicago, IL.

Fein, G., & Robertson, A. R. (1974). Cognitive and social dimensions of pretending in two-year-olds. (ERIC Document Reproduction Service No. ED 119 806).

Fein, G., & Rivkin, M. (Eds.). (1986). *The young child at play: Reviews of research* (Vol. 4). Washington, DC: National Association for the Education of Young Children.

Fein, G., & Schwartz, P. (1982). Developmental theories in early education. In B. Spodek (Ed.), *Handbook of research in early childhood education* (pp. 82–104). New York: The Free Press.

Fenson, L., & Ramsay, D. (1980). Decentration and integration of child's play in the second year. *Child Development, 51,* 171–178.

Fink, R. S. (1976). Role of imaginary play in cognitive development. *Psychological Reports, 39*, 895–906.

Fischer, J. L., & Fischer, A. (1963). The New Englanders of Orchard Town, U.S.A. In B. Whiting (Ed.), *Six cultures: Studies of child rearing* (pp. 869–1010). New York: John Wiley.

Fiske, E. B. (1986, May 27). Classes debated for 4-year-olds. *New York Times*, pp. 1, 10.

Florio, S., & Walsh, M. (1981). The teacher as colleague in classroom research. In H. T. Treubay, G. P. Guthrie, & K. Au (Eds.), *Culture and the bilingual classroom: Studies in classroom ethnography* (pp. 87–101). Rowley, MA: Newbury House.

Forman, G. (1985, April). *The child's understanding of record and replay in computer animated graphics.* Paper presented at the Annual Meeting of the American Educational Research Association, Chicago, IL.

Forman, G. E., & Hill,, F. (1980). *Constructive play: Applying Piaget in the preschool.* Monterey, CA: Brooks/Cole.

Forys, S., & McCune-Nicholich, L. (1984). Shared pretend: Sociodramatic play at three years of age. In I. Bretherton (Ed.), *Symbolic play: The development of social understanding* (pp. 159–194). Orlando, FL: Academic Press.

Foster, G. M. (1979). *Tzintzuntzan: Mexican peasants in a changing world.* New York: Elsevier.

Freud, A. (1964). *Psychoanalytic treatment of children* (N. Proctor-Gregg, Trans.). New York: Schocken Books.

Futrell, M. H. (1986, December). Restructuring teaching: A call for research. *Educational Researcher, 15*(10), 5–8.

Garvey, C. (1974). Some properties of social play. *Merrill-Palmer Quarterly, 20*, 163–180.

Garvey, C. (1977). *Play.* Cambridge, MA: Harvard University Press.

Garvey, C., & Berndt, R. (1977). Organization of pretend play (*JSAS Catalogue of Selected Documents in Psychology*, Manuscript 1589). Washington, DC: American Psychological Association.

Gelman, R. (1983). Recent trends in cognitive development. In J. Schierer & A. Rogers (Eds.), *The G. Stanley Hall lecture series* (Vol. 3) (pp. 145–175). Washington, DC: American Psychological Association.

Genishi, C. (1983, April). *Role initiation in discourse of Mexican-American children's play.* Paper presented at the annual meeting of the American Educational Research Association, Montreal, Canada.

Giffin, H. (1984). The coordination of meaning in the creation of a shared make-believe reality. In I. Bretherton (Ed.), *Symbolic play: The development of social understanding* (pp. 73–100). Orlando, FL: Academic Press.

Gilmore, P., & Glatthorn, A. A. (Eds.) (1982). *Children in and out of school.* Washington, DC: Center for Applied Linguistics.

Giroux, H. A., & McClaren, P. (1986). Teacher education and the policies of engagement: The case for democratic schooling. *Harvard Educational Review, 56*, 213–238.

Goffman, E. (1974). *Frame analysis.* New York: Harper & Row.

Goldman, J. A. (1981). Social participation of preschool children in same- vs. mixed-age groups. *Child Development, 52*, 644–650.

Golomb, C., & Cornelius, C. B. (1977). Symbolic play and its cognitive significance. *Developmental Psychology, 13*, 246–252.

Golomb, C., Gowing, E., & Friedman, L. (1982). Play and cognition: Studies of pretense play and conservation of quantity. *Journal of Experimental Child Psychology, 33*, 257–279.

Gould, R. (1972). *Child studies through fantasy: Cognitive-affective patterns in development.* New York: Quadrangle Books.

Green, J., & Wallat, C. (Eds.) (1981). *Ethnography and language in educational settings.* Norwood, NJ: Ablex.

Griffin, E. F. (1982). *Island of childhood: Education in the special world of nursery school.* New York: Teachers College Press.

Gumperz, J. (Ed.). (1982a). *Discourse strategies* (Vol. 1). Cambridge, England: Cambridge University Press.

Gumperz, J. (Ed.). (1982b). *Language and social identity* (Vol. 2). Cambridge, England: Cambridge University Press.

Harms, T., & Clifford, M. (1980). *The day care environment rating scale.* New York: Teachers College Press.

Hartup, W. W. (1983). The peer system. In P. H. Mussen & E. M. Hetherington (Eds.), *Handbook of child psychology: Vol. 4. Socialization, personality and social development* (pp. 103–196). New York: John Wiley.

Hendrickson, J., Strain, P., Tremblay, A., & Shores, R. (1981). Relationship between toy and material use and the occurrence of social interactive behavior by normally developing preschool children. *Psychology in the Schools, 18,* 500–504.

Hsu, F. L. K. (1970). *Americans and Chinese: Purpose and fulfillment in great civilizations.* New York: Natural History Press.

Hutt, C. (1971). Exploration and play in children. In R. E. Herron & B. Sutton-Smith (Eds.), *Child's play* (pp. 231–251). New York: John Wiley.

Isaacs, S. (1933). *Social development in young children.* London: Routledge & Kegan Paul.

Isaacs, S. (1966). *Intellectual growth in young children.* New York: Schocken Books. (Originally published 1930)

Jackowitz, E. R., & Watson, M. W. (1980). Development of object transformations in early pretend play. *Developmental Psychology, 16,* 543–549.

Johnson, J. E., & Ershler, J. (1981). Developmental trends in preschool play as a function of classroom program and child gender. *Child Development, 52,* 995–1004.

Joopnarine, J., & Mounts, N. (1985). Mother-child and father-child play. *Early Childhood Development and Care, 20,* 157–169.

Kamii, C., & DeVries, R. (1980). *Group games in early education: Implications of Piaget's theory.* Washington, DC: National Association for the Education of Young Children.

Katz, L. G. (1975, March). Early childhood programs and ideological disputes. *The Educational Forum, 39*(3), 267–271.

Kearney, M. (1972). *The winds of Ixtepeji: World view and society in a Zapotec town.* New York: Holt, Rinehart and Winston.

Kee, D. W. (1985). Computer play. In C. Brown & A. Gottfried (Eds.), *Play interactions: The role of toys and parental involvement in children's development* (Pediatric Roundtable, 11) (pp. 53–60). Skillman, NJ: Johnson and Johnson Baby Products.

Keliher, A. U. (1986, September). Back to basics or forward to fundamentals? *Young Children, 41*(6), 42–44.

Keller-Cohen, D. (1978). Context in child language. *Annual Review of Anthropology, 7,* 453–482.

Kessen, W., & Cahan, E. D. (1986). A century of psychology: From subject to object to agent. *American Scientist, 74,* 640–649.

Kohlberg, L., & Mayer, R. (1972). Development as the aim of education. *Harvard Educational Review, 42,* 449–496.

Kohlberg, L., Yaeger, I., & Hjertholm, E. (1968). Private speech: Four studies and a review of theories. *Child Development, 39,* 691–736.

Kritchevsky, S., & Prescott, E., with Walling, L. (1969). *Physical space: Planning environments for young children.* Washington, DC: National Association for the Education of Young Children.

Langlois, J., & Downs, A. (1980). Mothers, fathers and peers as socialization agents of sex typed behaviors in young children. *Child Development, 51,* 1237–1247.

Lather, P. (1986, August). Research as praxis. *Harvard Education Review, 56*(3), 257–277.

Lazar, I., & Darlington, R. (1982). Lasting effects of early education: A report from the Consortium for Longitudinal Studies. *Monographs of the Society for Research in Child Development, 47*(2–3, Serial No. 195).

Lieberman, J. N. (1977). *Playfulness: Its relationship to imagination and creativity.* New York: Academic Press.

Light, P. (1979). *The development of social sensitivity.* Cambridge: Cambridge University Press.

McCune, L. (1985). Play-language relationships and symbolic development. In C. Brown & A. Gottfried (Eds.), *Play interaction: The role of toys and parental involvement in children's development* (Pediatric Roundtable, 11) (pp. 38–44). Skillman, NJ: Johnson and Johnson Baby Products.

McCune, L. (1986). Symbolic development in normal and atypical infants. In G. Fein & M. Rivkin (Eds.), *The young child at play: Reviews of research* (Vol. 4) (pp. 45–61). Washington, DC: National Association for the Education of Young Children.

McCune-Nicolich, L. (1981). Toward symbolic functioning: Structure of early pretend games and potential parallels with language. *Child Development, 52,* 785–797.

McLoyd, V. (1980). Verbally expressed modes of transformation in the fantasy play of black preschool children. *Child Development, 52,* 1133–1139.

McLoyd, V. (1982). Social class differences in sociodramatic play: A critical review. *Developmental Review, 2,* 1–30.

McLoyd, V. (1983). The effects of the structure of play objects on the pretend play of low income preschool children. *Child Development, 54,* 626–635.

McLoyd, V. (1986). Scaffolds or shackles? The role of toys in preschool children's pretend play. In G. Fein & M. Rivkin (Eds.), *The young child at play: Reviews of research* (Vol. 4) (pp. 63–77). Washington, DC: National Association for the Education of Young Children.

Mead, G. H. (1934). *Mind, self and society.* Chicago: University of Chicago Press.

Mead, M. (1951). *Growth and culture.* New York: Putnam.

Miller, P., & Garvey, C. (1984). Mother-baby role play: Its origins in social support. In I. Bretherton (Ed.), *Symbolic play: The development of social understanding* (pp. 101–130). Orlando, FL: Academic Press.

Miller, S. N. (1974). The playful, the crazy, and the nature of pretense. In E. Norbeck (Ed.), *The anthropological study of human play. Rice University Studies* (Vol. 60) (pp. 31–51). Houston, TX: Rice University.

Minturn, L., & Lambert, W. (1964). *Mothers of six cultures: Antecedents of child rearing.* New York: John Wiley.

Monighan, P. (1985, April). *The development of symbolic expression in preschool play and language.* Paper presented at the annual meeting of the American Educational Research Association, Chicago, IL.

Monighan, P. (1986, April). *Parents and preschoolers report on home play patterns, television and pretending.* Paper presented at the annual meeting of the American Educational Research Association, San Francisco, CA.

Moore, N. V., Evertson, C. M., & Brophy, J. E. (1974). Solitary play: Some functional reconsiderations. *Developmental Psychology, 10,* 830–834.

Moore, S. G. (1977, November). Old and new approaches to preschool education. *Young Children, 33*(1), 69–72.

Mueller, E., & Brenner, J. (1977). The origins of social skills and interaction among play group toddlers. *Child Development, 48,* 854–861.

Mussen, P. H. (Ed.). (1970). *Carmichael's manual of child psychology* (Vols. 1 & 2). New York: John Wiley.

Mussen, P. H., & Hetherington, E. M. (1983). *Handbook of child psychology: Vol. 4. Socialization, personality, and social development.* New York: John Wiley.

National Association for the Education of Young Children. (1986, September). Position statements on developmentally appropriate practice in early childhood programs. *Young Children, 41*(6), 3–29.

Nelson, K., & Gruendal, J. (1979). At morning it's lunchtime: A scriptal view of children's dialogues. *Discourse Processes, 2,* 73–94.

Noddings, N., & Shore, P. (1984). *Awakening the inner eye: Intuition in education.* New York: Teachers College Press.

Nucci, L. P., & Turiel, E. (1978). Social interactions and the development of social concepts. *Child Development, 49,* 400–407.

Opie, I., & Opie, P. (1976). Street games: Counting-out and chasing. In J. S. Bruner, A. Jolly, & K. Sylva (Eds.), *Play: Its role in development and evolution* (pp. 394–412). New York: Basic Books.

Overton, W. F., & Jackson, J. P. (1973).The representation of imagined objects in action sequences: A developmental study. *Child Development, 44,* 309–314.

Paley, V. (1984). *Boys and girls: Superheroes in the doll corner.* Chicago: University of Chicago Press.

Parish, W., & Whyte, M. K. (1978). *Village and family in contemporary China.* Chicago: University of Chicago Press.

Parten, M. B. (1932). Social participation among preschool children. *Journal of Abnormal Psychology, 27,* 243–269.

Pederson, D. R., Rook-Green, A., & Elder, J. (1981). The role of action in the development of pretend play in young children. *Developmental Psychology, 17,* 756–759.

Pellegrini, A. (1980). The relationship between kindergartners' play and achievement in pre-reading, language and writing. *Psychology in the Schools, 17,* 530–535.

Pepler, D. J. (1982). Play and divergent thinking. In D. J. Pepler & K. H. Rubin (Eds.), *Contributions to human development: Vol. 6. The play of children: Current theory and research* (pp. 64–78). Basel, Switzerland: Karger.

Piaget, J. (1954). *The construction of reality in the child.* New York: Ballantine Books.

Piaget, J. (1962). *Play, dreams and imitation in childhood.* New York: W. W. Norton.

Piaget, J. (1965). *The moral judgment of the child.* New York: Free Press.

Piaget, J. (1969). *The language and thought of the child.* New York: World Publishing.

Pi-Sunyer, O. (1973). *Zamora: Change and continuity in a Mexican town.* New York: Holt, Rinehart & Winston.

Preschool enrollment at record high in U.S. (1986, October 15). *New York Times,* p. 20.

Pulaski, M. (1970). Play as a function of toy structure and fantasy predisposition. *Child Development, 41,* 531–537.

Ramos, S. (1962). *Profile of man and culture in Mexico.* Austin, TX: University of Texas Press.

Roberts, J. M., Arth, M., & Bush, R. R. (1959). Games in culture. *American Anthropologist, 61,* 597–605.

Roberts, J. M., & Sutton-Smith, B. (1962). Child training and game involvement. *Ethnology, 1,* 166–185.

Robinson, P. A., & Hom, H. (1979). Child psychology and early childhood education. In H. Hom & P. A. Robinson (Eds.), *Psychological processes in early education* (pp. 23–45). New York: Academic Press.

Roper, R., & Hinde, R. (1978). Social behavior in a play group: Consistency and complexity. *Child Development, 49,* 570–579.

Rubin, K. (1982). Non-social play in preschoolers: Necessarily evil? *Child Development, 53,* 651–657.

Rubin, K., Fein, G., & Vandenberg, B. (1983). Play. In P. H. Mussen, & E. M. Hetherington (Eds.), *Handbook of child psychology: Vol. 4. Socialization, personality and social development* (pp. 693–774). New York: John Wiley.

Rubin, K., Maioni, T. L., & Hornung, M. (1976). Free play behaviors in middle- and lower-class preschoolers: Parten and Piaget revisited. *Child Development, 47,* 414–419.

Rubin, K., Watson, K., & Jambor, T. (1978). Free play behavior in preschool and kindergarten children. *Child Development, 49,* 534–536.

Ruopp, R. (1985). Foreword. In J. T. Cook, *Child day care.* Davis, CA: International Dialogue Press.

Ryan, J. (1974). Early language development: Towards a communication analysis. In M. P. Richards (Ed.), *The integration of the child into a social world* (pp. 185–213). Cambridge: Cambridge University Press.

Saltz, E., Dixon, D., & Johnson, J. (1977). Training disadvantaged preschoolers on various fantasy activities: Effects on cognitive functioning and impulse control. *Child Development, 48,* 367–380.

Scarr, S., & Weinberg, R. (1986). The early childhood enterprise: Care and education of the young. *American Psychologist, 41*(10), 1140–1146.

Schank, R., & Abelson, R. (1977). *Scripts, plans, goals and understanding.* Hillsdale, NJ: Lawrence Erlbaum.

Schwartzman, H. B. (1977). Children's play: A sideways glance at make-believe. In D. F. Lancy & B. Allan Tindall (Eds.), *The anthropological study of play: Problems and prospects* (pp. 208–215). Cornwall, NY: Leisure Press.

Schwartzman, H. B. (1978). *Transformations: The anthropology of children's play.* New York: Plenum.

Schwartzman, H. B. (1984). Imaginative play: Deficit or difference? In T. Yawkey & A. Pellegrini (Eds.), *Child's play: Developmental and applied* (pp. 49–62). Hillsdale, NJ: Lawrence Erlbaum.

Schwartzman, H. B. (1985). Child-structured play: A cross-cultural perspective. In C. Brown & A. Gottfried (Eds.), *Play interactions: The role of toys and parental involvement in children's development* (Pediatric Roundtable, 11) (pp. 11–18). Skillman, NJ: Johnson and Johnson Baby Products.

Schweinhart, L. J., Weikart, D. P., & Larner, M. B. (1986). Consequences of three preschool curriculum models through age 15. *Early Childhood Research Quarterly, 1,* 15–45.

Shapiro, E., & Biber, B. (1972, September). The education of young children: A developmental-interaction approach. *Teachers College Record, 74*(1), 55–79.

Sigel, I. (1982). The relationship between parental distancing strategies and children's cognitive behavior. In I. Sigel & L. M. Laosa (Eds.), *Families as learning environments for children* (pp. 47–66). New York: Plenum Press.

Singer, J. (1973). *The child's world of make-believe.* New York: Academic Press.

Singer, J., & Singer, D. (1980). The values of imagination. In B. Sutton-Smith (Ed.), *Play and learning* (pp. 195–218). New York: Gardner Press.

Smilansky, S. (1968). *The effects of sociodramatic play on disadvantaged preschool children.* New York: John Wiley.

Smith, L. A. H. (1985). *To understand and to help: The life and works of Susan Isaacs (1885–1948).* Cranbury, NJ: Associated University Presses.

Smith, P. K. (1978). A longitudinal study of social participation in preschool children: Solitary and parallel play reexamined. *Developmental Psychology, 14,* 517–523.

Smith, P. K., & Dodsworth, C. (1978). Social class differences in the fantasy play of preschool children. *Journal of Genetic Psychology, 133,* 183–190.

Smith, P. K., & Dutton, S. (1979). Play and training in direct and innovative problem solving. *Child Development, 50,* 830–836.

Sponseller, L. (1982). Play in early education. In B. Spodeck (Ed.), *Handbook of research in early childhood education* (pp. 215–241). New York: Free Press.

Sroufe, L. A. (1979). The coherence of individual development: Early care, attachment, and subsequent developmental issues. *American Psychologist, 34,* 834–841.

Sroufe, L. A., & Waters, L. (1977). Attachment as an organizational construct. *Child Development, 48,* 1184–1199.

Steinbeck, J. (1969). "About Ed Ricketts," preface to *Log from the Sea of Cortez.* New York: Penguin Books. (Originally published 1941)

Stern, D. (1977). *The first relationship.* Cambridge, MA: Harvard University Press.

Suransky, V. P. (1982). *The erosion of childhood.* Chicago: University of Chicago Press.

Sutton-Smith, B. (1971). A syntax for play and games. In R. E. Herron & B. Sutton-Smith (Eds.), *Child's play* (pp. 298–307). New York: John Wiley.

Sutton-Smith, B. (Ed.). (1979). *Play and learning.* New York: Gardner Press.

Sutton-Smith, B. (1986). The spirit of play. In G. Fein & M. Rivkin (Eds.), *The young child at play: Review of research* (Vol. 4) (pp. 3–16). Washington, DC: National Association for the Education of Young Children.

Sutton-Smith, B., & Heath, S. B. (1981). Paradigms of pretense. *Quarterly Newsletter of the Laboratory of Comparative Human Cognition, 3*(3), 41–45. San Diego: Center for Human Information Processing.

Suzuki, K. (1983, April). *Effect of creative and idealized toys on children's play.* Paper presented at the biennial meeting of the Society for Research in Child Development, Detroit, Michigan.

Tizard, B., & Hughes, M. (1984). *Young children learning.* Cambridge, MA: Harvard University Press.

Tizard, B., Philips, J., & Plewis, I. (1976). Play in preschool centres II: Effects on play of the child's social class and of the educational orientation of the center. *Journal of Child Psychology and Psychiatry, 17,* 265–274.

Tucker, M., & Mandel, D. (1986, September). The Carnegie report — A call for redesigning the schools. *Phi Delta Kappan, 68*(1), 24–27.

Vandenberg, B. (1980). Play, problem solving and creativity. In K. H. Rubin (Ed.), *Children's play* (pp. 49–68). San Francisco: Jossey-Bass.

Vygotsky, L. S. (1962). *Thought and language.* Cambridge, MA: MIT Press.

Vygotsky, L. S. (1967). Play and its role in the mental development of the child. *Soviet Psychology, 12,* 62–76.

Waters, E., Wippman, J., & Sroufe, L. A. (1979). Attachment, positive affect, and competence in the peer group: Two studies in construct validation. *Child Development, 50,* 821–829.

Watson, M. W., & Fischer, K. W. (1980). Development of social roles in elicited and spontaneous behavior during the preschool years. *Developmental Psychology, 16,* 483–494.

Weber, E. (1984). *Ideas influencing early childhood education: A theoretical analysis.* New York: Teachers College Press.

Weisler, A., & McCall, R. (1976). Exploration and play. *American Psychologist, 31,* 492–508.

Werner, H., & Kaplan, B. (1964). *Symbol formation.* New York: John Wiley.

Wertsch, J. (1979). From social interaction to higher psychological processes: A clarification and application of Vygotsky's theory. *Human Development, 22,* 1–22.

Whiting, B. (1963). *Six cultures: Studies of child rearing.* New York: John Wiley.

Winnicott, D. W. (1971). *Playing and reality.* New York: Basic Books.

Wolf, M. (1968). *The house of Lim.* New York: Appleton-Century-Crofts.

Wright, H. F. (1960). Observational child study. In P. Mussen (Ed.), *Handbook of research methods in child development* (pp. 71–139). New York: John Wiley.

Wright, H. F. (1967). *Recording and analyzing child behavior with ecological data from an American town.* New York: Harper & Row.

Yawkey, T., & Pellegrini, A. (Eds.). (1984). *Child's play: Developmental and applied.* Hillsdale, NJ: Lawrence Erlbaum.

index

about the authors

Patricia Monighan-Nourot is assistant professor of education at Sonoma State University in Rohnert, California, where she teaches early childhood education. She began her graduate studies in education as a fellow in the Interdisciplinary Studies in Day Care and Child Development at the University of California, Berkeley. She continued there as teacher-director of the preschool while she pursued her Ph.D. in educational psychology. In 1981, she was selected as one of the state's ten outstanding preschool directors by the California Council of Parent Participation Preschools. Her interests in children's play and language extend, in addition to teaching, to research and consultation in the design of computer software for children.

Barbara Scales is head teacher at the Harold E. Jones Child Study Center at the University of California, Berkeley, where she took her Ph.D. in education. Prior to her current appointment, she worked as an arts consultant in Berkeley's alternative schools program, as director of a parent cooperative nursery school, and in the university art museum's Community Arts Project. An accomplished painter, she is interested in dramatic and visual art as self-reflecting modes of learning that have special potential in the study of human development.

Judith Van Hoorn is assistant professor of education at the University of the Pacific in Stockton, California, where she teaches child development and reading. She has worked on the development of science curricula in the United States and, as a Peace Corps volunteer, in Korea. She then worked as education coordinator for Head Start in San Joaquin County, California, and received her Ph.D. in education from the University of California, Berkeley. In addition to her work on children's play, she has conducted research and written extensively on the psychological effects of the nuclear threat on children. She is coeditor of *Growing Up Scared?* (1986), a volume on that subject.

Millie Almy is professor emerita at the University of California, Berkeley. She received her Ph.D. from Columbia University in New York, where she taught developmental psychology at Teachers College for many years. She began her career as a nursery school teacher, later becoming a supervisor and child care center director. She is author of numerous articles and books, including *The Early Childhood Educator at Work* (1975) and, with Celia Genishi, *Ways of Studying Children* (1979).